# Cultural and Diversity Issues in Counseling

## Edited by

**Paul B. Pedersen,**
*The University of Alabama at Birmingham*
**Don C. Locke,**
*North Carolina State University-Asheville*

**Introduction by Courtland C. Lee**

ERIC Counseling & Student Services Clearinghouse
School of Education • 101 Park Building
University of North Carolina at Greensboro
Greensboro, North Carolina • 27412-5001

ERIC/CASS Publications
School of Education
University of North Carolina at Greensboro
Greensboro, NC  27412-5001


ISBN 1-56109-071-9


This publication was funded by the U.S. Department
of Education, Office of Educational Research and
Improvement, Contract no. RR93002004. Opinions
expressed in this publication do not necessarily
reflect the positions  of the U.S. Department of
Education, OERI, or ERIC/CASS.

# Preface

*Garry R. Walz*

No greater challenge exists for counselors today than that of developing their own personal conception of and approach to multicultural counseling. It is difficult to even conceive of a more compelling topic or one that offers more potential benefits to a counselor and her/his clients.

The importance of and interest in multiculturalism is attested to by the large number of publications that are available. The large quantity however can be as confusing as helpful to a counselor aspiring to be both better informed and more competent. It was therefore only after considerable study and review that we decided to proceed, but with the clear goal of offering a publication that filled a special need—that of assisting counselors to develop their own personal approach to multicultural counseling based on a clear understanding of the issues, the needs, and special interventions appropriate to different subcultures.

Drs. Pedersen and Locke have done a masterful job of selecting an array of knowledgeable and eloquent writers. Additionally they have greatly added to the worth and utility of the publication through their own cogent and compelling contributions. The broad sweep of this publication plus the specific information it provides on working with clients of different cultures insures that it will be read and used over and over again.

I congratulate Drs. Pedersen, Locke and their fellow authors for this unique contribution to the counseling literature. It will undoubtedly prove highly beneficial to counselors and those they seek to help. We also are highly appreciative of the thoughtful introduction by Dr. Courtland Lee. It is a significant contribution to the monograph.

Garry R. Walz, Ph.D.,NCC
Director and Senior Research Scientist, UNCG
Professor Emeritus, University of Michigan

# Introduction

*Courtland C. Lee*

I am extremely honored to write the introduction to this book. I have known Drs. Pedersen and Locke as respected colleagues and valued friends for many years. I have also had the opportunity to collaborate with a number of the chapter contributors on various professional projects. All of the individuals involved with this book have a keen understanding that cultural issues are critically important and challenging to counseling. Scores of professional counselors seem to be ill prepared to provide culturally responsive counseling services to diverse populations. Many are searching for new ways to intervene successfully into the lives of people from a variety of cultural backgrounds. This search is made even more urgent by demographic projections that suggest that cultural diversity will have an even greater impact on American society in the rapidly approaching 21st century.

The search for multicultural counseling effectiveness has led to the publication of a spate of books devoted to this issue in recent years. While all of these books have been a variation on a theme, each in its own way has advanced the theory and practice of multicultural counseling. This book, therefore, joins a growing number of books that expand the knowledge base in the important discipline of multicultural counseling. While this book bears striking similarities to others in the field, Pedersen and Locke and their contributors offer the profession some important new perspectives on diversity issues in counseling. These new perspectives were no doubt motivated by the senior editor's provocative notion that *multiculturalism* represents the "fourth theoretical force" in counseling, building on psychodynamic, cognitive/behavioral, and humanistic theories.

It is obvious from the controversies associated with culture-centered counseling discussed in the first chapter that this book takes a somewhat different slant on multicultural counseling. The ten controversies presented here represent the essence of what I have called "the promise and pitfalls of multicultural counseling." The authors have done an outstanding job of synthesizing the major issues and challenges associated with counseling across cultures. I have no doubt that the ten controversies discussed by Pedersen and Locke will stimulate continued dialogue and debate about the nature of multicultural counseling.

The chapters in the first part of the book are an examination of specific ethnographic cultures. This part of the book will be the most familiar to anyone who has examined similar scholarly works on multicultural counseling. There are the obligatory chapters on counseling the "major" ethnic minority groups (i.e., American Indians, Asian Americans, African Americans, and Hispanics). Each of these chapters follows a now familiar format of providing a demographic and/or psychosocial profile of each group and, in most instances, a case study which emphasizes critical issues for culturally responsive counseling. However, the editors have gone beyond the familiar to include chapters on the Amish and Appalachian Whites. In addition, there is a fascinating chapter on counseling Chamorros, people who trace their cultural origins to Guam and the Northern Marianas. I found this chapter to be particularly fascinating because it introduced me to a cultural group of which I had no knowledge. This chapter brought home for me again how complex the concept of culture is and the ever-expanding nature of diversity in North America. As professional counselors we all still have much to learn about our clients and fellow Americans.

The first part of the book is made the more impactful by the inclusion of a chapter on White racism. This is an extremely important chapter. Most multicultural counseling books imply the notion of White racism or pay lip service to the concept. This book examines the issue in a scholarly, but "head-on" fashion. It is important that professional counselors understand that they will not be effective with culturally diverse clients until they examine and confront their own preconceived notions and prejudicial assumptions that foster racist attitudes and behaviors. This is particularly true for White counselors, since they continue to represent the majority of those in the profession and also enjoy cultural privilege in American society. The comprehensive model of racism presented in this chapter offers counselors direction in dealing with their own racism and helps to focus efforts on challenging it at a societal level. This chapter will definitely "push your buttons," regardless of your racial heritage.

The second part of the book, however, is what truly sets this book apart from most others in the multicultural counseling field. This section goes beyond the concept of "multiculturalism" as merely race or ethnicity. It deals with demographic, status, and affiliation cultures. These run the gamut from athletes to spiritual and religious cultural groups. These chapters lend credence to a broad definition of culture and the idea that all counseling relationships are cross-cultural in nature.

While some may argue that identifying athletes, individuals with brain injuries, or homeless people as "cultural groups" may stretch the concept of culture somewhat thin, the authors of these chapters write convincingly and compellingly about the dynamics of these groups. After reading these chapters and the others in this section of the book it is obvious that we must consider any group of people who identify with each other on the basis of some common purpose, need, or similarity of background as a distinct cultural group.

After reading about issues in counseling Buddhist individuals, people with HIV, and people with disabilities, I was left to wonder how many

other demographic, status or affiliation groups the counseling profession fails to respond to in culturally sensitive ways. This section of the book raised my level of awareness to cultures I had never considered and certainly broadened my thinking about the nature of multicultural counseling.

The work of Paul Pedersen, Don Locke, and their contributors in this book makes a significant addition to the literature on multicultural counseling. It is not just another book on counseling across cultures. They have helped to advance the knowledge base on culture in counseling practice with their efforts. This book provides a major stimulus for the development of greater awareness about the importance of cultural responsiveness in counseling practice. It provides a wider lens through which to view culture and its relationship to counseling theory and practice. The ideas presented here are an important effort in freeing multicultural counseling from the exclusive, and often narrow, confines of race and ethnicity. Pedersen and Locke's work offers a counseling framework which provides equal access and opportunities to all people.

In my opinion, this book also represents the first effort in the next generation of scholarly work in the discipline of multicultural counseling. The editors and their contributors invite us to think "outside of the box" when it come to issues of culture and counseling. I applaud them for the efforts. I encourage you to turn the page.

July 12, 1996

Courtland C. Lee
Professor of Counselor Education
University of Virginia

# Foreword

*Paul B. Pedersen & Don C. Locke*

Counseling has been culturally diversified for a very long time, but only in recent years have the providers of counseling become aware of their clients' cultural diversity. With increased visibility and awareness of cultural and diversity issues in counseling, several things have happened. First, the field of counseling has become more aware of the client's perspective, which is frequently, if not always, culturally different from the counselor's perspective. Second, as assessment measures have increasingly attended to diversified cultural contexts those measures have become more accurate. Third, the curriculum of counselor education has been revised to reflect issues of culture and of diversity. Fourth, counselors in practice have had to re-educate themselves regarding cultural and diversity issues. This book is intended to meet the needs of these changes in the field of counseling by reviewing concerns arising from an emphasis on culture and diversity in counseling.

Counseling as an approach to individual or social problems was a product of Euro-American applications of psychology to practical social issues. With increased urbanization and with the help of increased technology in the industrialized world, the ability of family and natural support groups to deal with personal problems was reduced—the field of counseling was invented to deal with those problems. As the rest of the world has become industrialized and modernized, the same problems arise and counseling is being "re-invented" to address those problems. As a result of adapting counseling to a variety of new environments, several controversies have entered the debate. As we begin the process of looking at cultural and diversity issues it may be useful to consider some of these controversies.

## Controversies

The first controversy involves the continuing encapsulation of counseling as a professional field (Wrenn, 1962). Cultural encapsulation means that:

1. reality is defined by narrow assumptions,
2. cultural variations among individuals are minimalized to a dominant culture,
3. evidence disconfirming the superiority of the dominant culture is disregarded,
4. technique-oriented strategies and short-term solutions are preferred, and
5. others are judged according to the encapsulated person's self-reference criteria.

Wrenn (1985) suggested that the incidence of cultural encapsulation is increasing among counselors. This conclusion is confirmed by Albee (1994) who describes the fundamental assumptions of psychology as limited to the Euro-American cultural perspective. Pedersen (1994) identifies 10 specific examples of underlying culturally learned assumptions which demonstrate encapsulation. Sue and Sue (1990) discuss the importance of status-quo maintenance by encapsulated counselors. Ponterotto and Casas (1991) describe how encapsulated assumptions limit the effectiveness of counseling efficacy based on research data.

The second controversy relates to the continued use of culturally biased assessments and measures. Lonner and Ibrahim (1989) review specific ways in which counseling assessments are culturally biased. Any unbiased measure would need to account for each client's world view, specific norms, and should include standardized as well as clinical aspects. The standardized assessments now available fail to distinguish between constructs and criteria, do not establish equivalence, can not accomodate both verbal and nonverbal stimuli, avoid response sets, infer deficits from test scores, and embed Westernized preference. These biases contribute to overdiagnosis, underdiagnosis, or misdiagnosis (Dana, 1993; Paniagua, 1994). The search for culture-free or even culture-fair tests has failed (Escobar, 1993). Lonner (1990) points out that testing and assessment methods are culture-specific based on psychological constructs not universally accepted. This makes equivalence difficult to achieve in assessment, favors verbal over nonverbal behaviors, and results in classifying cultures in superior/inferior relationships.

The third controversy relates to whether culture should be defined broadly or narrowly. The broad definition of culture presumes that any ethnographic, demographic, status, or affiliation variable may be potentially salient in defining one's "cultural" identity. According to this broad definition all counseling is multicultural, given the complex pool of potentially salient cultural identities for each individual. Segal, Dasen, Berry, and Poortinga (1990) describe culture inclusively as the totality of whatever all persons learn from other persons. Culture gives meaning to the changing environment (Shweder, 1990), which may include social class (Goldstein, 1994), political identity (Sampson, 1993), and avoidance of rigid stereotypes (Sue and Sue, 1990).

Triandis, Botempo, Keung, and Hui (1990) distinguish among cultural, demographic, and personal constructs, reserving "cultural" for those who speak the same dialect, live in the same geographic area, and share a similar "ethnography." Lee (1991) argues that the broad definition is so inclusive it becomes meaningless and Locke (1990) suggests that the broad definition of culture has diffused the coherent conceptual framework of multiculturalism in training, teaching, and research.

The fourth controversy involves measuring ethno-racial-cultural identity. These measures are based on a conceptual framework proposed by Thomas (1971) on a six-stage "negromachy" and confirmed independently by Cross (1971) in a four-stage "nigrescence" framework of Black

identity development. Jackson (1975) also introduced a Black identity development model with four stages. Marcia (1980) applied Erikson's stages of crisis in ego identity formation and Delworth (1989) then applied this composite to gender-related aspects of identity development. Helms (1985) synthesized the previous models into a stage model based on five assumptions:

1. Minority groups develop model personality patterns in response to White racism;
2. Some styles of identity are more healthy than others;
3. Cultural identity requires new attitudes toward cognitive, affective, and behavioral processes;
4. Styles of identity are distinguishable; and
5. Cultural interaction is influenced by the participant's cultural identity.

Helms (1990) traces identity development from a pre-encounter stage where the Black idealizes White standards and then either ignores or is assimilated into a White society. In the second encounter stage the Black is confronted with racial injustice. The third immersion stage follows an internalized but stereotyped Black perspective. The fourth stage of internalization moves toward a positive Black identity, and the final stage involves commitment to a positive internalized perspective. Cross (1991) modified his earlier theory and Helms' synthesis to include a "thoughtful shift of salience" from a convergent nationalistic to a more divergent multicultural perspective of "internalization-commitment" as the final stage. The measurement of ethno-cultural identity continues to evolve.

The fifth controversy is between those who would emphasize similarities and those who would emphasize differences. Pike (1966) originallly borrowed from the field of linguistics the term "phonemics," (emic) referring to sounds unique in a particular language, and the term "phonetics" (etic) or universal language sounds. The emic/etic distinction has led some to emphasize group differences and others to highlight group similarities, while both ignore the essential complementarity of both aspects. Brewer (1991) described social identity as a tension between nomothetic similarity and unique individuation, while, at the same time, holding a dual emphasis. Segall, et al.(1990) also combine similarities and differences beginning with an "imposed etic" working from within one's own cultural viewpoint "as though" it were a universal rule while refining and adapting those rules in practice to local differences toward a "derived etic." The emic approach has fallen into the trap of relativism encapsulating each group and excluding outsiders, while the etic approach has been associated with universalism and the melting pot which deprives groups of their identity and imposes the culture of the more powerful.

The sixth controversy involves the ethical responsibility to do the right thing. Given the American Counseling Association's and American Psychological Association's cultural bias in professional ethical guidelines, the multicultural counselor may be forced into "responsible disobedience" in order to do the right thing (Casas & Thompson, 1991; Pedersen & Marsella, 1982). The professional ethical guidelines emphasize a counselor's ethical responsibility to know their client's cultural values before delivering a service, but those same professional guidelines each continue to support the narrow perspective of a dominant culture in their underlying—and unstated and unacknowledged—assumptions (Pedersen, 1994). Professional ethical guidelines seem more concerned with protecting providers against culturally different consumers (Axelson, 1993; Corey, Corey, & Callanan, 1993; LaFromboise & Foster, 1989; Pontorotto & Casas, 1991). The professional ethical guidelines seem to escape into abstract generalizations in the unstated assumption that all counselors of good will share the same cultural assumptions. Seeking safety in abstractions allows individual counselors to project their own self-referenced cultural assumptions on the guidelines at the expense of culturally different clients (Pedersen, 1995).

The seventh controversy entails the training of counselors in a culture-centered perspective. Culture-centered training of counselors requires a shift from simplistic to more complex thinking about multiple and overlapping cultural identities, all within an "orthogonal" model of counseling (Oetting and Beauvais, 1991). The trained counselor has a wider response repertoire to fit each different complex and dynamic client context. Several training models have been suggested. Ridley, Mendoza, and Kanitz (1994) describe Multicultural Counseling Training (MIT) as a framework moving from philosophy to objectives. Landis and Brislin (1983) describe training that divides experiential/discovery approaches from didactic/expository approaches. Sue, Arredondo, and McDavis (1992) outline a three-stage developmental sequence from awareness to knowledge to skill. It is increasingly clear that training approaches which minimalize or trivialize culture by including a token course in their curriculum are inadequate. The culture-centered perspective is being recognized as generic and fundamental to all aspects of counselor training and not just to working with exotic populations. Remodeling the curriculum for counselor education toward a culture-centered approach is necessary for accurate assessment, meaningful understanding, and appropriate intervention.

The eighth controversy consists of the tension between a culture-general and a culture-specific view in defining the theory and practice of counseling. The functional precursors of counseling have been around for a long time although the labels of "counseling" and "therapy" are relatively new. Counseling has spread with the rise of urbanization and industrialization to countries and cultures where "talk therapy" is a least preferred source of help and support. Psychology has assumed that there is somehow a "fixed state of mind" whose observation is obscured by cultural distortion. Psychology has assumed a single, universal, and culture-general definition of normal behavior whatever the client's culture. Anthropology, on the other hand assumed that cultural differences are clues to divergent attitudes, values, and perspectives in a culture-specific understanding of normal behavior. Anthropologists have taken the relativist position when classifying behaviors across cultures while Psychologists have minimized diverse cultural viewpoints. Each of these two contrasting perspectives complements the other (Pedersen, in press).

The ninth controversy comprises the domination of westernized values in counseling. The "westernized" perspective is not grounded in geography but is rather a socio-political perspective present in both Western and non-Western geographical regions. Westernized theories presume that each individual is separate, independent and autonomous, and guided by traits, abilities, and values different from others. Western cultures are described by Berry et al. (1992) as more idiocentric, emphasizing competition, self-confidence, and freedom, whereas non-Western cultures are more allocentric, emphasizing communal and collectivistic responsibility, social usefulness, and the acceptance of authority. Westernized beliefs grew out of a naturalistic understanding of the physical world of the Enlightenment in Europe, where human behavior was objectively understood in terms of "mass and extension" rather than through internalized and more subjective categories (Taylor, 1989). The contrast between westernized and non-westernized thinking is most apparent in majority/minority cultural relationships, resulting in "scientific racism" and Euro-American ethnocentrism (Pedersen, Fukuyama, & Heath, 1989). Increased attention to "indigenous psychology" (Kim & Berry, 1993) has focused study on non-Western perspectives resulting from international contact, postcolonial relationships, internationalizing the social sciences, radicalization of special interest groups, activism of social scientists, interdisciplinary cooperation, and a methodological paradigm shift (Sloan, 1990).

The tenth controversy relates to the paradigm shift toward multiculturalism as a "fourth force" to supplement psychodynamic, behavioral, and humanist counseling perspectives. Wrightsman (1992) describes this shift toward collectivist thinking in a bottom-up consumer-driven demand similar to Kelly's personal construct theories. The social constructivist perspective is based on the premise that we do not have direct access to a singular, stable, and fully knowable external reality but rather that we depend on culturally embedded, interpersonally connected, and necessarily limited notions of reality. McNamee and Gergen (1992) have applied this framework to counseling to understand a client's subjective reality within his or her cultural context. Reality, according to this newly emerging contextual and constructivist view, is not based on absolute truth but on complex and dynamic relationships in a cultural context and is not understood abstractly but through relationships in context (Steenbarger, 1991). Claiborn and Lichtenberg (1989) also emphasize the sociocultural context for "interactional counseling" where change is reciprocal and multidirectional and where each event is both cause and effect. The new paradigm requires the inclusion of more subjective constructivist and contextual data based on the sociocultural context of a multiculturally diverse society.

## Conclusion

Cultural and diversity issues are central to the field of counseling. The importance of multiculturalism has been largely overlooked because it is consumer driven rather than the product of any single, expert individual. The multicultural revolution is a bottom-up and not a top-down revolution in the field of counseling. For that reason, many times the consumers of counseling services are more aware of this rapidly changing focus than the providers. This does not mean that the multicultural emphasis intends to replace other theories, but rather that it attempts to guide the theory and practice of counseling toward a more culture-centered foundation. The objective of the movement is not just to establish multiculturalism as a new guild, but to increase the excellence of counseling generally. The culture-centered perspective is not "subtractive," competing with other theories, but is "additive" in facilitating more effective counseling from every viewpoint and in every context.

It is hoped that the following chapters will generate many questions for readers. These chapters are not directed toward easy answers; instead, they guide the reader toward understanding the complicated and dynamic cultural forces which mediate the effectiveness of counselors working with culturally different clients.

# References

Albee, G. W. (1994). The sins of the fathers: Sexism, racism and ethnocentrism in psychology. *International Psychologist, 35* (1), 22.

Axelson, J. A. (1993). *Counseling and development in a multicultural society.* Pacific Grove, CA: Publisher.

Berry, J. W., Poortinga, Y. H., & Dasen, P. J. (1992). *Cross cultural psychology: Research and applications.* Cambridge, England: Cambridge University Press.

Brewer, M. B. (1991). The social self: On being the same and different at the same time. *Personality and Social Psychology Bulletin, 17,* 475-482.

Casas, J. M., & Thompson, C. E. (1991). Ethical principles and standards: The racial ethnic minority perspective. *Counseling and Values, 35,* 186-195.

Claiborn, C. D., & Lichtenberg, J. W. (1989). Interactional counseling. *The Counseling Psychologist, 71,* 355-453.

Corey, G., Corey, M. S., & Callanan, P. (1993). *Issues and ethics in the helping professions* (4th ed.). Pacific Grove, CA: Brooks/Cole.

Cross, W. (1971). The negro-to-Black conversion experience. *Black Worlds, 20,* 13-17.

Cross, W. (1991). *Shades of black.* Philadelphia: Temple University Press.

Dana, R. H. (1993). *Multicultural assessment perspectives for professional psychology.* Boston: Allyn & Bacon.

Delworth, U. (1989). Identity in the college years: Issues of gender and ethnicity. *Journal of National Association of Student Personnel Administrators, 26,* 162-166.

Escobar, J. E. (1993). Psychiatric epidemiology. In A. C. Gaw (Ed.), *Culture, ethnicity and mental illness* (pp. 43-73). Washington, DC: American Psychiatric Press.

Goldstein, A. (1994). Teaching prosocial behavior to low-income youth. In P. Pedersen & J. Carey (Eds.) *Multicultural counseling in schools* (pp. 157-176). Boston: Allyn & Bacon.

Helms, J. E. (1985). Cultural identity in the treatment process. In P. Pedersen (Ed.), *Handbook of cross-cultural counseling and therapy* (pp. 239-245). Westport, CT: Greenwood Press.

Helms, J. E. (1990). *Black and white racial identity: Theory, research and practice.* Westport, CT: Greenwood Press.

Jackson, B. (1975). Black identity development. In L. Golubschick & B. Persky (Eds.) *Urban social and educational issues* (pp. 158-164). Dubuque, IA: Kendall-Hall.

Kim, U., & Berry, J. W. (1993). Introduction. In U. Kim & J. W. Berry, *Indigenous psychologies: Research and experience in cultural context.* Newbury Park, CA: SAGE.

LaFromboise, T. D., & Foster, S. L. (1989). Ethics in multicultural counseling. In P. Pedersen, J. Draguns, W. Lonner, and J. Trimble, *Counseling across cultures* (3rd ed. , pp. 115-136). Honolulu, HI: University of Hawaii Press.

Landis, D., & Brislin, R. W. (1983). *Handbook of intercultural training: Volume I issues in theory and design.* New York: Pergamon Press.

Lee, C. C. (1991). Promise and pitfalls of multicultural counseling. In C. C. Lee & B. L. Richardson (Eds.), *Multicultural issues in counseling: New approaches to diversity* (pp. 1-13). Alexandria, VA: American Association for Counseling and Development.

Locke, D. C. (1990). A not so provincial view of multicultural counseling. *Counselor Education and Supervision, 30* (1), 18-25.

Lonner, W. (1990). An overview of cross-cultural testing and assessment. In R. W. Brislin, *Applied cross-cultural psychology.* (pp.56-76). Newbury Park, CA: SAGE.

Lonner, W. J., & Ibrahim, F. A. (1989). Assessment in cross-cultural counseling. In P. Pedersen, J. Draguns, W. Lonner, & J. Trimble (Eds.), *Counseling across cultures* (3rd ed.) (pp. 229-334). Honolulu, HI: University of Hawaii Press.

Marcia, J. E. (1980). Identity in adolescence. In J. Adelson (Ed.), *Handbook of adolescent psychology* (pp. 159-187). New York: Wiley.

McNamee, S. & Gergen, K. J. (1992). *Therapy as social construction.* Newbury Park, CA: SAGE.

Oetting, E. R., & Beauvais, F. (1991). Orthogonal Cultural Identification Theory. The cultural identification of minority adolescents. *The International Journal of the Addictions, 25,* 655-685.

Paniagua, F. A. (1994). *Assessment and treatment of multicultural groups in mental health practices: A practical guide.* Newbury Park, CA:

Pedersen, P. (1994). *A handbook for developing multicultural awareness.* Alexandria, VA: American Counseling Association.SAGE.

Pedersen, P. (1995). Culture-centered ethical guidelines for counselors. In J. G. Ponterotto, J. M. Casas, L. A. Suzuki, & C. M. Alexander, *Handbook of multicultural counseling* (pp. 34-49). Thousand Oaks, CA: SAGE.

Pedersen, P. (in press). *Culture-centered counseling interventions: The search for accuracy.* Thousand Oaks, CA: SAGE.

Pedersen, P., Fukuyama, M. A., & Heath, A. (1989). Client, counselor and contextual variables in multicultural counseling. In P. Pedersen, J. Draguns, W. Lonner, & J. Trimble (Eds.), *Counseling across cultures* (3rd ed., pp. 23-53). Honolulu, HI: University of Hawaii Press.

Pedersen, P., & Marsella, A. C. (1982). The ethical crisis for cross-cultural counseling and therapy. *Professional Psychology, 13,* 492-500.

Pike, R. (1966). *Language in relation to a united theory of the structure of human behavior.* The Hague: Mouton.

Ponterotto, J. G., & Casas, J. M. (1991). *Handbook of racial/ehtnic minority counseling research.* Springfield, IL: Charles C. Thomas.

Ridley, C. R., Mendoza, D. W., & Kanitz, B. E. (1994). Multicultural training: Reexamination, operationalization and integration. *The Counseling Psychologist, 22* (2), 227-289.

Sampson, E. E. (1993). Identity politics: Challenges to psychology's understanding. *American Psychologist, 48* (12), 1219-1230.

Segall, M. H., Dasen, P. R., Berry, J. W., & Poortinga, Y. H. (1990). *Human behavior in global perspective: An introduction to cross-cultural psychology.* New York: Pergamon.

Shweder, R. A. (1990). Cultural psychology— What is it? In J. W. Stigler, R. A. Shweder, & G. Herdt (Eds.), *Cultural psychology: Essays on comparative human development* (pp. 73-112). New York: Cambridge University Press.

Sloan, C. (1990). Psychology for the Third World? *Journal of Social Issues, 46,* 1-20.

Steenbarger, B. N. (1991). All the world is not a stage: Emerging contextualist themes in counseling and development. *Journal of Counseling and Development, 70* (2), 288-296.

Sue, D. W., Arredondo, P., & McDavis, R. J. (1992). Multicultural counseling competencies and standards: A call to the profession. *Journal of Counseling and Development, 70,* 477-486.

Sue, D. W., & Sue, D. (1990). *Counseling the culturally different: Theory and practice.* New York: Wiley Interscience.

Taylor, C. (1989). *Sources of the self: The making of the modern identity.* Cambridge, MA: Harward University Press.

Thomas, C. (1971). *Boys no more.* Beverly Hills, CA: Glencoe Press.

Triandis, H. C., Botempo, R., Leung, K., & Hui, C. H. (1990). A method for determining cultural demographic and person constructs. *Journal of Cross-Cultural Psychology, 21,* 302-318.

Wrenn, C. G. (1962). The culturally encapsulated counselor. *Harvard Educational Review, 32,* 444-449.

Wrenn, C. G. (1985). Afterward: The culturally encapsulated counselor revisited. In P. Pedersen (Ed.), *Handbook of cross-cultural counseling and therapy* (pp. 323-329). Westport, CT: Greenwood Press.

# Table of Contents

# Ethnographic
# Cultures

# African American Women: Status and Counseling Implications

*Patricia Y. Leonard*

## Abstract

This article presents an overview of the status of African American women. Issues associated with counseling interventions with this group are discussed. It includes a demographic and socioeconomic profile, summary of unique stresses and problems, and implications for counseling and research. A case study is provided to illustrate major concepts.

## Overview

African American women have by virtue of their race and gender occupied a unique and often marginal position in our society. Counseling interventions must be responsive to the diverse backgrounds and issues presented by this population.

## Demographic and Socioeconomic Profile

Bureau of the Census (1993) data on the 16.7 million African American women indicate that:

1. African American women are more likely than their Caucasian counterparts to live without a male partner than with one. Thirty-eight percent of those over age 14 were married, 39% had never married, 11% were divorced, and 11% widowed.
2. Forty-six percent of African American households which were responsible for 54% of African American children were female-headed.
3. Sixty-seven percent of African American women completed high school and 12% earned at least bachelors degree. These rates were comparable to those of African American men but lower than those of Caucasians.
4. Fifty-eight percent of African American women were classified as in the labor force.
5. The median income of African American women employed full-time ($18,720) was lower than that of their male counterparts and Caucasian women and men.
6. In 1991 the median family income of African American female headed families with no spouse present was $11,410; that for similar Caucasian families was $19,550.
7. Seventy-eight percent of the 2.3 million African American families living in poverty in 1991 were headed by single women.

## Special Problems

Racism and discrimination have hindered equitable access of African Americans to opportunities for education, employment, and those aspects of life related to socioeconomic status such as personal safety, quality housing, medical care, and overall quality of life. The marginal status of African Americans within American society is exacerbated for African American women who are the objects of the "double whammy" (i.e., race and gender). A detailed review of research on the psychological functioning of African American women is beyond the scope of this article, however some key issues are summarized. Smith (1982) and Jeffries (1976) identify many positive indicators of well-being including high levels of self-esteem, aspiration, and self-reliance. They also note high levels of commitment to others and less rigid gender based stereotypes. Jackson and Sears (1992) mention resourcefulness, resilience, support systems, and prayer as some of the coping strategies of African American women.

In spite of many positive characteristics and coping strategies, African American women are prime candidates for mental illness (including depression and schizophrenia) and are most often treated for psychological disorders (Smith, 1985) during their prime (25–44 years). Jackson and Sears (1992) identify multiple roles, poverty, high demands and limited resources, racism, dominant culture ethnocentrism, sexism, and oppressive social conditions as factors contributing to high levels of stress experienced by African American women. Suicidal behavior and alcoholism are increasing among African Americans in general and particularly among African American women who attempt suicide at younger ages and in greater proportions than Caucasian women (Smith, 1985). Diagnoses reflecting greater degrees of psychopathology (Cannon & Locke, 1977) and tendencies toward premature withdrawal from treatment (Sue, McKinney, Allen, & Hall, 1974) are noted.

### Stressors

Poverty is a primary stressor for many African American women. Poverty-based stresses include overcrowded and substandard living arrangements, financial instability, welfare dependence, limited medical care, greater exposure to crime, and a sense of powerlessness. For generations many African American women have been employed outside the home and assumed the primary financial and custodial responsibility for the care of minor children and aging relatives. Most work for wages outside their homes due to economic necessity related either to the absence of a male figure in the family support structure or to lower earning levels of the supporting male partner. Many of these women are concentrated in occupational areas which typically provide little internal satisfaction, little status, little opportunity for advancement, and meager pay. The demands of multiple roles in a "mainstream" environment characterized by gender bias and marginal access and acceptance make them prime candidates for role strain and depression.

Allowing for some alteration of viewpoints over the past two decades, it is probable that many African American women have maintained the traditional family-life views discussed by Helms (1979) and are troubled by the likelihood of spending a considerable portion of their lives as single women or single parents. Wilkinson (1984) provides a discussion of African American women and selected family variables. While many African American women have extended family structures and support networks which might ameliorate life stresses, an abundance of stressful events in the lives of network members may compromise rather than enhance the client's psychological well-being.

Available research concerning the nature and extent of psychological distress suffered by African American women leaves many unanswered questions. While many cope admirably against difficult circumstances, many suffer greatly from the ravaging social, psychological, and economic by-products of racism and gender bias.

### Implications for Counseling Practice

The heterogeneity among African American women with respect to socioeconomic circumstances, lifestyle, social/psychological support system, educational attainments, degree of acculturation, and psychological strength is a paramount consideration in their treatment. While elements of the Africentric (sic) perspective (Priest, 1991; Jackson, 1985; Jackson & Sears, 1992) may be applicable to the client's world view, their relevance should be assessed rather than assumed. Brown-Collins and Sussewell (1986) present a model based on the interactive effects of racism, sexism, and individual difference to describe the self-concept of African American women. The model includes psychophysiological (self as woman), African American (sociopolitical) and myself (personal history) referents. Assessing the unique world view of an African American woman entails consideration of her views of self and perceptions of her social, cultural, and economic reality; as well as her values and beliefs. Counseling should include exploration and validation of the client's experiences with racism and sexism and their impact on various aspects of her life. An attitude of respect and pattern of suspended judgment of the client's world view should prevail as the client's concerns, phenomenological world, environmental context, degrees of acculturation and alienation, and coping methods are assessed. Africentric (sic) concepts described by Jackson and Sears (1992) which include emphasis on communal orientation;

cooperation rather than confrontation, control, and competition; flexible time perspective; harmony with nature; self-knowledge; and spiritual faith may facilitate understanding of some African American women.

Counselors must not ignore the possibility that the client's problems are not necessarily nor entirely intrapersonal and be willing to consider the impact of environment and to work toward systemic (environmental) changes. Respect for the client's experiences, perceptions, and positive attributes may move her toward greater degrees of empowerment. A supportive relationship and early impact with respect to the issues presented by the client are critical to developing motivation for continued commitment to counseling. Initial efforts directed toward acknowledgment and resolution of presenting issues can contribute to the client's sense of empowerment, respect and commitment. The introduction of counselor identified issues should be tentative, well-timed and presented as related to client identified concerns. Problem assessment and goal setting must recognize environmental barriers and resources, as well as personal issues and strengths.

An eclectic approach allows the counselor to develop case conceptualizations and interventions which address the client's unique issues and style. Education, problem solving, insight, behavioral, expressive, experiential, cognitive and other approaches may all be useful in efforts to provide culturally sensitive counseling for African American women. Approaches including reframing of experience in accordance with aspects of the Africentric (sic) world view may promote a greater sense of well-being among some women (Jackson & Sears, 1992).

## Implications for Counseling Research

Research which includes descriptive and explanatory inquiries of psychological functioning, career aspirations and behavior, and life coping modalities is needed. By identifying promising counseling interventions for specific client status and problem variables, and by including diversity among demographic and other critical life variables, counselors could expand knowledge beyond prevailing stereotypical and monolithic views of African American women.

## Case Study

Kai, a 27 year old divorced African American woman with three children, was referred to counseling by her employer for poor job performance and absenteeism. Initial assessment sessions revealed substantial depression, low self-esteem, and negative perceptions of work situation and life circumstances. Recent stressful life events include the death of her mother, a job termination, and an unpleasant attempt to share a home with a younger sister and her children. Her most recent "setback" was the termination of a relationship which she hoped would lead to marriage and greater security. Drained financially and emotionally by her efforts to care for her mother and to help other family members, she is embittered and wearied by the struggles of life. She perceives little reward for her efforts and feels powerless to improve things.

Kai's world view was a complex amalgamation of Africentric (collective, affiliative, interdependent, and cooperative personal orientation) and Eurocentric (competitive, acquisitive, and individualistic) perspectives and values. Perceptions that aspects of her environment (i.e., poverty, inferior education, racism, lack of suitable partners) inhibited her quest for "fulfillment" were initially accepted to facilitate formation of a therapuetic relationship.

The primary goal was to work through conflicting values, beliefs, and perceptions to arrive at a system (world view) in which Kai could feel optimistic about her future. Making life changes consistent with the revised world view was the second major goal. Early attention to issues which Kai felt were most critical (resolution of workplace and family pressures) increased her commitment to counseling. The treatment was eclectic. Gestalt, Person Centered, and Adlerian approaches developed affective awareness, self-understanding, self-acceptance, and closure on losses. Stress management and cognitive and behavioral self-modification strategies increased her self-efficacy and optimism. Existential and Cognitive Behavioral techniques assisted Kai in reflecting on aspects of her life and in solidifying a more focused value system. Reframing of experience afforded her a new more self-affirming perspective on many issues. Counseling outcomes included increased understanding of self and environment, enhanced coping skills, greater sense of direction and control, and decreased depression.

## References

Belle, D. (Ed.). (1982). *Lives in stress.* Beverly Hills, CA: Sage.

Brown-Collins, A. R., & Sussewell, D. R. (1986). The Afro- American woman's emerging selves. *Journal of Black Psychology, 13,* 1-11.

Bureau of the Census (1993). *The Black population of the United States: March 1992.* Washington, D.C.: United States Department of Commerce.

Cannon, M.S., & LockeB.Z. (1977). Being Black is detrimental to one's mental health: Myth or reality? Phylon, 408-428.

Helms, J. A. (1979). Black women. *The Counseling Psychologist, 8,* 40-42.

Jackson, A. P. (1993). Black, single working mothers in poverty: Preferences for employment, well-being, and perceptions of preschool-age children. *Social Work, 38,* 26-34.

Jackson, A. P. & Sears, S. J. (1992). Implications of an Africentric worldview in reducing stress for African American women. *Journal of Counseling and Development, 71,* 184-189.

Jackson, G. G. (1985). Cross-cultural counseling with Afro-Americans. In Pedersen, P. (Ed.) *Handbook of cross-cultural counseling and therapy.* Westport, CN: Greenwood Press.

Jeffries, D. (1976). Counseling for the strengths of the Black woman. *The Counseling Psychologist, 7,* 20-22.

Priest, R. (1991). Racism and prejudice as negative impacts on African American clients in therapy. *Journal of Counseling and Development, 70,* 213-215.

Smith, E. J. (1982). The Black female adolescent: A review of educational, career, and psychological literature. *Psychology of Women Quarterly, 6,* 261-262.

Smith, E. J. (1985). Counseling Black women. In Pedersen, P. (Ed.), *Handbook of cross-cultural counseling and therapy.* Westport, CN: Greenwood Press.

Sue, S., McKinney, H. Allen, D., & Hall, J. (1974). Delivery of community mental health services to Black and White clients. *Journal of Consulting and Clinical Psychology, 42,* 794-801.

Wilkinson, D. Y. (1984). Afro-American women and their families. *Marriage and Family Review, 7,* 125-142.

Wortman, R. A. (1981). Depression, anger, dependency, denial: Work with poor, Black, single parents. *American Journal of Orthopsychiatry, 36,* 662-669.

# American Indian and Alaska Native Mental Health

*Teresa D. LaFromboise & Kate E. Young*

### Overview

The 1990 census counted 1,878,000 American Indians and Alaska Natives. Native American Indians are extraordinarily ethnically diverse. There are over 450 identifiable tribal units. The smallest tribes may have as few as four or five remaining enrolled members. The largest tribe, the Navajo of New Mexico and Arizona, has over 170,000 members (Trimble & Medicine, 1993). There are 200 tribal languages still spoken. The tribal social and religious functions, structures, and ceremonies remain intact in many communities. Despite these facts there is the tendency for Indians to be "museumized" in the minds of many people in the dominant culture. Indian people are often thought of as belonging to remnants of bygone eras. Native Americans often feel pressure to assert their presence because to most Americans they are invisible, unlike African Americans, Asian Americans, Hispanics, and Latinos.

The Native American population appears to be growing. The 1990 census of almost 1.9 million is up from fewer than 1.4 million in 1980, a 38% growth rate. This rise is due to the increasing willingness of Americans of Indian ancestry to identify their race as Indian on census forms (Fost, 1991). More than 60% of people who identify themselves as Native American are from mixed Indian and African American, Euro-American, or Hispanic backgrounds (Trimble & Medicine, 1993). The population is geographically dispersed with a concentration of Indian people living primarily in ten states: Oklahoma, California, Arizona, New Mexico, Alaska, Washington, North Carolina, Texas, New York, and Michigan. Currently, more than half of the Native American population resides in suburban and urban areas. The population is also fluid with many thousands more using the reservation as a principal residence but spending varying amounts of time off the reservation, either seeking education and employment, visiting relatives, or finding respite from stresses in their home communities (Fleming, 1992).

Native Americans continue to face cultural genocide. They have suffered tremendous, social, spiritual, emotional, and economic losses since the arrival of non-Indians to America. It is necessary to understand the social and historical context of the Native American population in order to appreciate fully what is both very positive and tragic in the current demographics. Before extensive contact with Europeans in 1500, some 2.5 million indigenous people lived in what is now the United States. Yet by 1890, only 250,000 of this population remained. The 1990 census of almost 1.9 million is still less than the estimated before-contact population. Non-Indians tend to discount the impact that this traumatic history has on the problems in Indian communities. Indians on reservations face consistently high rates of unemployment and have the lowest average rates of educational attainment of any ethnic group in the United States (Ward, 1995). Delinquency rates of Native Americans are among the highest of any ethnic minority group in the country. When alcohol-related offenses are factored out, delinquency rates are comparable to those of Anglo and Hispanic people (Duclos, LeBeau, & Elias, 1994).

The social and economic stresses faced by Native Americans are manifold. Like all minority populations in the United States, they face the stress of individual and institutionalized racism. Many Indians also face bicultural pressures to retain their traditions in the face of a dominant culture that has either attacked, denigrated, or exploited them. Another disturbing reality is the prevalence of premature deaths due to accidents, homicide, and suicide among young adults, as well as premature death due to inadequate health care and nutrition. Eleven percent of Indian youth have experienced the death of a parent (Blum, Harmon, Harris, Bergeisen, & Resnick, 1992.) The median age of both American Indians (20.4 years) and Alaska Natives (17.9 years) is significantly younger than the population in general (30.3 years) (US Department of Commerce 1983.) Only 10% of Indians and Alaska Natives are aged 55 and over. Consequently, there are few within the elder generation to guide the family, community, and tribe, a void that is keenly felt given the high value placed on the wisdom of elders (Red Horse, 1980).

Confusion about gender roles also causes conflict and stress. Traditionally, men and women had gender-specific tasks and responsibilities and the contributions of each gender were equally esteemed. Indian women can still fulfill their traditional roles as caretakers and transmitters of culture. Indian men, on the other hand, have few opportunities to fulfill their traditional roles. For example, little need now exists for hunters and warriors. Non-Indian sex-role stereotypes and expectations have disrupted the complementarity of male and female roles. Native American women now face sexism from both the dominant society and from Indian men.

The family is an essential part of Native American life. Traditional Indian families are composed of extensive networks of people. Family networks may include several households consisting of relatives along vertical and horizontal lines, and may include non-kin, such as clan members. Relatives are expected to teach young people life skills, and grandparents often share in child-rearing responsibilities (Red Horse, 1981). This family structure provides a sense of groundedness not often available in urban settings. Returning frequently to reservations to visit relatives and to participate in social and spiritual events helps maintain this network. The current household structure has changed significantly for some Indians. Recent research shows that 45% of Indian homes are headed by women, and 42% of those women are under the age of 20 when they have their first child. Many never marry (Snipp & Aytac, 1990). This loss of the extended family

both contributes to and exacerbates stress. Intertribal marriages are common among Native Americans, as are mixed-race marriages. Mixed-race marriages have an additional strain, that of threats to their children's Indian identity.

Native Americans have shown impressive reservoirs of strength and ability in coping with persistent hardships, yet most communities reflect the degree to which these problems have taken a toll. High levels of alcohol and other substance abuse, plus disturbed family and interpersonal relationships, including domestic violence, sexual assault, child physical and sexual abuse, and child neglect (Neligh, 1988) have contributed to the high rates of mental health disorders associated with social stress. The most common mental health problems are major depression, anxiety, and adjustment reactions, which often co-occur with alcohol and other substance dependence or abuse. Post-traumatic stress disorder, difficulties in family relationships, and somatic complaints are also common. Finally, grief related to on-going loss of freinds and family is a major contributor to psychological disturbance and difficulty.

The first source of help sought by Indian people is the extended family; the second source is spiritual leaders and tribal community leaders. The mainstream health care system is approached as a last resort (Lewis, 1984). However, some reports show mental health service utilization in urban settings is increasing (O'Sullivan, Peterson, Cox, & Kirkeby, 1989) and the stigma attached to mental health treatment is decreasing (Kahn, Lejero, Antone, Francisco, & Manuel, 1988). This change could be related to greater Indian involvement in mental health care. A number of barriers prevent Indians from obtaining needed mental health care. One, there are few Indian counselors and psychologists. Between 1985 and 1990, only four Indians completed doctoral programs in Clinical and Counseling Psychology (Trimble, 1991). Further, not all of these Ph.D.s do direct clinical work with Indians. The Indian Health Service (IHS), the primary deliverer of mental health services to Indians, is aware of the need for more culturally-sensitive mental health services on reservations, yet very few Indian psychologists choose to work there.

Family focused interventions hold promise if the willing participation of all the members of the family can be obtained. This may be difficult because of the issues of privacy and the reluctance to open up family businesses to outsiders. However, some clinicians have reported success with family therapy, especially when traditional and Western therapeutic practices are integrated (Tafoya, 1989; Topper & Curtis, 1987). Culturally sensitive group interventions fit well with many tribes' social and political emphasis on group interaction and consensus. Successful psychoeducational group programs have focused on decreasing alcohol abuse (Wolman, 1970), treating the sexual abuse of Indian girls (Ashby, Gilchrist, & Miramontez, 1987), and teaching parenting skills (BigFoot, 1989). Additional groups address smoking cessation, substance abuse, pregnancy prevention among youths (Schinke et al., 1988), and suicide prevention (LaFromboise & Howard-Pitney, 1994; 1995).

Communities have begun to develop their own interventions (Swinomish Tribal Mental Health Project, 1991). One shining example is the Alkali Lake community's achievement of a 97% sobriety rate in 15 years (Willie, 1989). The elements of this successful transformation were a commitment by core tribal members to sobriety, with strong tribal leadership using native and non-native resources. Members also confront the role of non-Indians in maintaining drinking in the community as well as Indians taking responsibility for their own actions. A focus on spiritual needs and a focus on caring for and nurturing one another was primary. This intervention has changed the community norm of non-interference in the case of severe alcohol abuse.

An increasing number of Indians are seeking individual psychotherapy. When they seek services, these interactions are affected by the cultural emphasis on non-directness in communication and a stance of non-interference in interpersonal relationships. These are often misinterpreted by non-Indian clinicians as resistance or as a sign that the Indian client is not a good candidate for change in psychotherapy. The bicultural or nontraditional Indian client may be more receptive to mental health services. The following case study illustrates a client's efforts at separating her own unresolved issues from issues she is having with her adolescent daughter. The value of non-interference and non-directness can be seen in this case.

## Case Study

Mary, an Indian woman in her mid-40's, and her non-Indian husband operated a ranch on her reservation allotment, and they enjoyed a comfortable income. Mary also worked in a rest home as an LPN in a nearby town bordering the reservation. Her children attended integrated schools in that town, and they had both done well academically and socially. Over the years, Mary and her husband encouraged their children to participate in tribal and community organizations, such as an Indian dance group and 4-H club.

Mary presented herself at a mental health clinic for support during a time when she and her daughter, age 16, were in extreme conflict. Mary's daughter had been dating an older, non-Indian adolescent who had a reputation for drug abuse. During the previous year Mary's son, age 18, had been to peer counseling training in the area of chemical dependence prevention, and the entire family had participated in the associated family program. She was proud of her son's growth and grateful for the opportunities the family had had to learn and heal together. Mary was anxious about her daughter's choice of friends and feared that she and her husband would lose the closeness with their daughter that they had had, especially in recent months (Trimble & Fleming, 1985, pp. 196-197).

There is a strong need for research on the process of social support among Indians of various ages and backgrounds. Longitudinal studies would be particularly useful in identifying the antecedents of social isolation and the potency of various sources of cultural and social support for Indian clients and their families. Also, attention to the coping styles and life-styles of Indians with varying levels of Indian affiliation is necessary to shift the focus away from deficit hypotheses to the design of interventions that build on the "natural" strengths of Indian people and communities.

To date, there is only one study of Indian preferences for counseling style (Dauphinais, Dauphinais, & Rowe, 1981). This study questioned the efficacy of neo-Rogerian helping approaches. There is also a need for studies concerning the impact of social influence variables, such as trustworthiness and perceived status of the counselor on counseling outcomes with Indian clients. More knowledge about the relevance and effectiveness of various interview techniques, such as reflection, confrontation and self-disclosure, and about facilitating the counseling relationship with Indian clients would also be helpful.

Often, clinicians believe that they will have little or no contact with Native Americans because there are not large concentrations of Indians in their area. However, Native Americans can be found in virtually every state, although their numbers are small in some instances. Counselors must be willing to seek out Indians and discover the Native Indians' definition of health and community in order to find ways to best serve them.

## References

Ashby, M. R., Gilchrist, L. D, & Miramontez, A. (1987). Group treatment for sexually abused American Indian adolescents. *Social Work with Groups, 10*, 21-32.

BigFoot, D. S. (1989). Parent training for American Indian families. *Dissertation Abstracts International, 50*, 1562A. (University Microfilms No. AAC 89-19982).

Blum, R. W., Harmon, B., Harris, L., Bergeisen, L, & Resnick, M. D. (1992). American Indian-Alaska Native youth health. *Journal of the American Medical Association, 266*(12), 1637-1644.

Dauphinais, P., Dauphinais, L., & Rowe, W. (1981). Effects of race and communication style on Indian perceptions of counselor effectiveness. *Counselor Education and Supervision, 21*, 72-80.

Duclos, C., LeBeau, W., & Elias, L. (1994). American Indian adolescent suicidal behavior in detention environments: Cause for continued basic and applied research. In *Calling from the rim: Suicidal behavior among American Indian and Alaska native adolescents* (Monograph 4, pp. 189-214).

Fleming, C. M. (1992). American Indians and Alaska Natives: Changing societies past and present. In M.A. Orlandi (Ed.), *Cultural competence for evaluators* (pp. 147-171). Washington, DC: US Department of Health and Human Services.

Fost, D. (1991). American Indians in the 1990s. *American Demographics, 13*, 26-34.

Kahn, M. W., Lejero, L., Antone, M., Francisco, D., & Manuel, J. (1988). An indigenous community health service on the Tohono O'odham (Papago) Indian reservation: Seventeen years later. *American Journal of Community Psychology, 16*, 369-379.

LaFromboise, T.D., & Howard-Pitney, B. (1994). The Zuni Life Skills Development Curriculum: A collaborative approach to curriculum development. *American Indian and Alaska Native Mental Health Research, The Journal of the National Center Monograph Series, 4*, 98-121.

LaFromboise, T. D., & Howard-Pitney, B. (1995). The Zuni Life Skills Development Curriculum: Description and evaluation of a suicide prevention program. *Journal of Counseling Psychology, 42*(4).

Lewis, R. (1984). The strengths of Indian families. *Proceedings of Indian child abuse conference.* Tulsa, OK: National Indian Child Abuse Center.

Neligh, G. (1988). Major mental disorders and behavior among American Indiansand Alaska Natives. *American Indian and Alaska Native Mental Health Research* (Monograph 1, pp. 116-159.)

O'Sullivan, M. J., Peterson, P. D., Cox, G. B., & Kirkeby, J. (1989). Ethnic populations: Community mental health services ten years later. *American Journal of Community Psychology, 17*, 17-30.

Red Horse, J. G. (1980). American Indian elders: Unifiers of Indian families. *Social Casework, 61,* 490-493.

Red Horse, J. G. (1981). American Indian families: Research perspectives. In F. Hoffman (Ed.), *American Indian Family: Strength and Stressors* (pp. 1-11). Isleta, NM: American Indian Social Research and Development Associates.

Schinke, S. P., Orlandi, M. A., Botvin, G. J., Gilchrist, L. D., Trimble, J. E., & Locklear, V. S. (1988). Preventing substance abuse among American Indian adolescents: A bicultural competence skills approach. *Journal of Counseling Psychology, 35,* 87-90.

Snipp, C. M., & Aytac, I. A. (1990). The labor force participation of American Indian women. *Research in Human Capital and Development, 6,* 189-211.

Swinomish Tribal Mental Health Project. (1991). *A gathering of wisdoms: Tribal mental health: A cultural perspective.* Mount Vernon, WA: Veda Vangarde.

Tafoya, T. (1989). Circles and cedar: Native Americans and family therapy. In *Minorities and family therapy* (pp. 71-96.), New York: Hawthorne House.

Topper, M. D., & Curtis, J. (1987). Extended family therapy: A clinical approach to the treatment of synergistic dual anomic depression among Navajo agency-town adolescents. *Journal of Community Psychology, 15,* 334-348.

Trimble, J. E. (1991). The mental health service and training needs of American Indians. In H. F. Meyers, P. Wohlford, L. P. Guzman, & R. J. Echemendia (Eds.), *Ethnic minority perspectives on clinical training and services in psychology* (pp. 43-48). Washington, DC: American Psychological Association.

Trimble, J. E., & Fleming, C. M. (1985). Providing Counseling Services for Native American Indians: Client, Counselor and Community Characteristics. In P. Pedersen (Ed.), *Handbook of Cross-cultural Counseling and Theories* (pp. 177-204). Westport, CT: Greenwood.

Trimble, J. E., & Medicine, B. (1993). Diversification of American Indians: Forming an Indigenous Perspective. In U. Kim & J. W. Berry (Eds.), *Indigenous Psychologies* (pp. 133-151). Newbury Park, CA: Sage.

U.S. Department of Commerce, Bureau of the Census. (May, 1983). *1980 census of population: Characteristics of the population* (U.S. Summary, PC 80-1-B1). Washington, DC: US Government Printing Office.

Ward, C. (1995, May). *Recent trends in educational attainment and employment among American Indians and Alaska Natives.* Paper prepared for the Workshop on the Demography of American Indian and Alaska Native Populations, Population Committee, National Research Council, Washington, D.C.

Willie, E. (1989). The story of Alkali Lake: Anomaly of community recovery or national trend in Indian country? *Alcoholism Treatment Quarterly, 6* (3/4), 167-174.

Wolman, C. (1970). Group therapy in two languages, English and Navajo. *American Journal of Psychotherapy, 24,* 677-685.

# Old Order Amish

*Joe Wittmer*

### Overview

This brief unit, written with deepest respect for my Amish heritage, is an attempt to reveal to the non-Amish "world" some of the genuine virtues of the Old Order Amish. The Old Order Amish Americans have been largely overlooked by historians and social scientists. Authors who have written about the Amish generally view them as a people of great integrity and goodwill, but have often exploited their uniqueness and picturesqueness. This unit is concerned with their positive, genuine values, and ways and customs as observed by myself as a former Amish sect member for 16 years.

The term "Amish" in this digest refers to the horse-and-buggy-driving, no-church-house, German-speaking sect often referred to as the "plain people." No attempt has been made to write about the Mennonites, Beachy's, Black Car Amish, nor other Amish offshoot groups.

It is difficult to pinpoint the exact number of Old Order Amish in America today. However, we do know that almost 24,000 children were enrolled in Amish schools (grades one through eight—no one goes beyond grade eight) during 1993-94. Thus, I estimate somewhere around 150,000 Old Order Amish living in the USA with probably another 10 or 15 thousand more living in Canada and South America. The Amish are expected to double in number every 15-20 years.

### Brief Description

The values of calmness, peace, total nonviolence and humility are in evidence in any Amish community. These values, practiced by the Amish adults, gain the allegiance of the Amish youth and few permanently leave the sect. Further, there is no indigence, divorce, or unemployment and very little delinquency.

The Amish want no part of the values and ways that exist in the modern world about them. They wish to be left alone to live their lives away from the mainstream of the secular society and they strive continually to remain different from the "other people," the "outsider," or the "English" as non-Amish are called. They shun the use of television, radio, telephone, and most other modern technological luxuries. Their plain homes lack running water, electricity, refrigerators, and most other modern conveniences. They converse amongst themselves in a German dialect and they wear home-sewn garbs, reminiscent of eighteenth century Quakers.

### Amish Order

The Amish sect was born out of the religious turmoil of the Anabaptist movement in sixteenth-century Europe. Their emergence was turbulent and they were a unique group during that time in history. They made it clear to both church and state that they would stop taking oaths, and would never again pick up a sword. However, the major difference between the Anabaptists and the other religious groups at that time in history was their feeling that baptism was not to be administered in infancy, but should occur when the person was old enough to reason. The Anabaptists were denounced as being heretics and hundreds were subjected to the death penalty.

The first Amish came to America at the invitation of William Penn and settled in the Penn colony around 1737. No Amish remain in Europe today.

### Problems with Modern-Day America

The most pressing problem facing the Amish in modern America, for which there appears no solution, is tourism. This is especially so in Lancaster County Pennsylvania where more than 20,000 tourists a day swarm over the Amish back roads creating havoc for the gentle Amish by taking their picture, endangering their lives with their fast cars, etc. Tourism is of little value to the Amish but it is a definite threat to their way of life.

Urbanization is threatening the Amish ways. This is especially true as farming becomes more mechanized and real estate developers send up the price of land. The economic problems of a people committed to a primitive technology, but imbedded in a highly technological society with which it must make exchanges across system lines, are immeasurable. In some areas, Amish are cooperating to buy farms by providing each other interest free loans. And in response, more and more "outsider" farm auctions are being held on Sunday, eliminating the cooperative Amish bidders.

Many Amish are now being forced to work in factories, etc. Industrial work is a departure from tradition made necessary by the changing economy. In time, factory work will no doubt erode some of the values the Amish have so long treasured. Factory work is especially detrimental to the close knit Amish family organization.

Local, state, and national legislators often pass new laws without the consent, knowledge, or consideration of different minority groups. A case in point is a law that has passed in several states requiring a triangular-shaped, reflectorized emblem to be affixed to the back of all slow-moving vehicles (the SMV). The Amish, in most states, view this three-cornered gaudy orange emblem as a hex symbol, or "the mark of the beast" as described in the Bible and have refused to affix it to their buggies. They further believe that the colorful emblem would glorify man rather than God. The Amish offer to use neutral colored reflector tape in an attempt at compromise, but such efforts often fail and many end up serving jail terms.

Local governments often build paved roads through Amish communities which bring fast cars and camera-toting (photos are forbidden) tourists to the Amish farmlands. These roads also play havoc to horses' feet. A horse simply cannot be continually driven on concrete, but local governments have not seen fit to leave grassy strips on either side of the new roads for the Amish

to use.

Non-Amish youth frequently invade the Amish communities at night and perform such harassments as turning out livestock, upsetting outdoor toilets, and burning corn and wheat shocks. This is especially prevalent during Halloween. The Amish are finding that it is difficult not to be "modern man" in today's world; many other problems facing them could be given here (Wittmer, 1991).

### Counseling the Old Order Amish Child

What role does public education play in the threat to the Amish way of life? In the past, most Amish communities were content to send their children to the local public elementary schools and it is estimated that some 4,000 still attend today. However, the emphasis on science and evolution, the increase of violence and drug usage, and educational TV have contributed to a sudden increase in the number of Amish parochial elementary schools.

The counselor who is effective with Amish children will be genuine and empathic, but also will follow the guidelines presented below:

1. De-emphasize the concept of self. The Amish child is taught to be cooperative rather than competitive, innovative, or aggressive. To the Amish, a child is not a unique individual. He or she is simply one member of a God-fearing group and should be treated as such.

2. Recognize the limitations of tests. Imagine the frustration of taking a test that requires you to identify a gas tank being removed from beneath a car, a well-known cartoon character, or a particular control dial on an electrical appliance when you've never seen them before.

3. Speed is rarely stressed in the Amish culture and children are admonished by their elders to do careful, accurate work. Amish children are told to work steadily and to do well what one does, rather than do a great deal and make careless mistakes. Children are taught never to skip anything that they do not understand.

They are to ponder it, to work at it, until they have mastered it. Thus, a teacher or counselor who administers a speed test to an Amish child could increase unnecessary psychological stress and fail to gain a true picture of the child's skill.

4. Understand culturally different groups' varied worlds of work. The world of work of Amish children is rather limited and neither children nor parents are interested in career exploration. These children emulate the work roles of Amish adults and want to be farmers or farmers' wives.

5. Respect the need for social distance that Amish children have with non-Amish children. A real concern among Amish parents today is the possibility that their children will form close, personal friendships with non-Amish children and become too comfortable with the ways of the outside world before they totally understand their own Amishness. Any attempt on the counselor's part to have Amish children form friendships (such as mixed group counseling) with non-Amish children will be contrary to the wishes of Amish parents.

6. Avoid probing into home or Amish community problems. Because institutions such as the home and the church are held in high esteem, Amish children enjoy participation within these institutions. The possibility of bringing shame on their family will inhibit talking about family or cultural problems. An Amish adult would never seek the services of a professional counselor.

7. Realize that a caring relationship is not enough. Affective understanding alone is not sufficient when counseling Amish children. The effective counselor also will be knowledgeable of the customs, traditions, and the values existing in the Amish child's unique environment.

8. Accept the fact that an Amish child's parents may have asked him or her to avoid counselors. Amish parents are responsible for training their children and consider themselves accountable to God for doing it correctly. Thus, your counseling or talking with them concerning values or morals may appear disrespectful to an Amish parent.

### Conclusion

To be an effective counselor with an Amish child in any setting you will need to use all of your counseling tools as well as learn all you can about the values and ways of the Amish culture and to keep your own cultural biases in check.

It is difficult to measure the total effect that America's progress has on a people such as the Amish who are committed to a primitive technology in the midst of a modern world bent on secularization. However, the Amish are a tenacious people and are intent; they will maintain their way of life.

### References

Wittmer, J. (1991). *The gentle people: Personal reflections of Amish life.* Minneapolis: Educational Media Corporation.

# Southern Appalachians: Ethnicity Obscured by Exploitation

*Hettie Lou Garland*

### Overview

The southern area of the Appalachian mountains includes West Virginia and the mountainous regions of Alabama, Georgia, Kentucky, North Carolina, Tennessee, and Virginia. Geographic, social, and economic isolation of Southern Appalachia was preserved until the advent of regional industrialization following the Civil War. The postwar need for fossil fuel and the expansion of the national economy fueled exploration of the region's wealth of timber and minerals. Coal mining and other economic prospects fostered increased access to the region and led to its discovery by others. People came to enjoy the beauty of the mountains and to increase their kowledge about Appalachia's inhabitants (Eller, 1982; Keefe, 1986; Mortensen, 1992).

By the end of the nineteenth century, hundreds of short stories and travelogues had been published about the region and its residents. Fiction was more appealing than fact, leading to descriptions of groups of people created by urban imaginations. Southern Appalachians were called hillbillies and were described as rude, awkward, primitive, impoverished, illiterate, violent, retarded, and isolated from the rest of the country. Fiction and continued exploitation of the stereotypes were the primary sources of information about native Appalachians until the middle of the twentieth century (Eller, 1982; Mortensen, 1992).

While these negative images have persisted, historians and researchers have begun to replace the stereotypes with accurate descriptions of the ethnic characteristics of Southern Appalachians. Southern Appalachians are defined as those who identify the region as their birthplace and whose families have lived in the mountains for at least three generations. Cultural values and characteristics include independence, self-reliance, identification with family and kinship networks, egalitarian orientation, and a strong belief in the will of God, which may lead to a fundamental spirituality and a sense of fatalism. Southern Appalachians exhibit adherence to specific standards of behavior, are hospitable, and may be shy around strangers, which is often misinterpreted as arrogance or indifference. They also exhibit self-reliance, endurance, and hard work. Southern Appalachians will fiercely defend their religious, social, or political rights in pursuing their way of life, which includes questions of how they may use their property (Williams, 1961; Eller, 1982; Keefe, 1986; Keefe, 1992).

The persistence of stereotypes concerning Southern Appalachians has created significant problems. Many Southern Appalachians have internalized the values and characteristics portrayed in the stereotypes, believing that they can only relate with outsiders on the basis of assumptions and myths. Internalization of stereotypes have led to a lack of self-confidence, a poor self-image, dependence, and an erosion of pride in their heritage and traditions. Unfortunately, health and human service programs may have been designed in accordance with these assumptions and myths. While the concept of blaming the victim is not restricted to mountaineers, solutions or assistance with some of these Appalachians' challenges have focused more often on changing the mountaineer, rather than on working within the cultural context. Social services are frequently based on models of social class, with an emphasis on poverty, or on rural residence, which in turn ignores urban Southern Appalachians (Keefe, 1986, 1992).

Keefe (1986) proposed the model of ethnicity as the most appropriate model both for cultural analysis and in planning or implementing social service programs. Her model included three areas of ethnicity: structural ethnicity, such as, social networks or socioeconomic class, refers to the obligation and opposition of the group within society; cultural ethnicity, such as, language or religion, describes the pattern of traits or attributes of the group; and, symbolic ethnicity, such as, attachment to the land, emphasizes the identification of group members with each other and their perceived differences from other groups. While these characteristics may be shared with other groups, Keefe argued that the holistic expression of difference, as well as the historical domination and stereotyping of Southern Appalachians by outsiders, defined Appalachians' distinct ethnicity.

Mental health programs, developed on models of ethnicity, provide counseling and other services within the cultural context. Successful counselors incorporate several principles in their work with this group:

*Accessibility.* The majority of Southern Appalachians live in rural areas, where geography and distance to urban centers limit time and travel. However, accessibility also applies to urban dwellers, who may share socioeconomic restrictions with their rural neighbors. Satellite clinics in remote rural or urban areas foster utilization and support the perception of reaching out. Local health departments, schools, churches, or other gathering places are ideal sites for outreach programs.

*Language.* There are real and perceived barriers in understanding the myriad of dialects and patterns of communication among Southern Appalachians. Successful counselors will learn to communicate with regional residents without talking down to them, and will avoid perceptions of "putting on airs" or trying to act or talk like one of them. Counselors may assist teachers, for instance, in understanding patterns of communication, using language as one strategy for fostering positive self-images and pride in cultural traditions.

*Definitions of health and illness.* Southern Appalachians continue to rely on self-diagnosis, defining illness in its interference with the ability to work or maintain daily activities. Reliance on home remedies, sharing of medications, and seeking professional care late in the progression of disease may characterize the use of health services. Physicians, nurses, or lay midwives are utilized more often than mental health professionals. Counselors must be able to recognize signs and symptoms of physical illness to assure timely referrals, thus building trust and confidence in the community.

*Religion.* Illness, disability, and death are often determined to be the will of God. Mountaineers are predominately Protestant, fundamental, and strongly influenced by belief systems. Excluding or ignoring religious influence in establishing therapeutic goals is the most common mistake of counselors. The power of prayer, forgiveness of sins, and the laying on of hands must be recognized as legitimate treatment strategies. Seeking mental health care may signal spiritual weakness or a disregard for the power of God. Counselors will be most successful, when they teach appropriate skills to clergy and lay church leaders and when they incorporate religious systems into therapeutic plans.

*Natural support systems.* Family and kinship networks provide natural, powerful support systems. These networks forge strong bonds for individuals, security, personal identity, role models, and reliable sources of help with problems. Families have community reputations; opportunities may be given, or failures overlooked because of family status. The definition of community is dynamic and not restricted to regional geography. Consequently, counselors may have several options in empowering these support systems.

Family systems may become enmeshed, eroding individual boundaries. One person's problems become everyone's problems. For instance, the cultural tradition of sitting up with the dead has been transported to waiting rooms in health care agencies, where extensive networks gather in times of crisis. Therapeutic goals may fail if family therapy or consultation with a family member is not considered. Crisis intervention will maladaptive coping patterns of the extended network are ignored (Eller, 1982; Keefe, 1986, 1992).

The successful counselor will provide care within the cultural context, replacing prejudice and stereotypes with knowledge and appreciation of the unique ethnicity of Southern Appalachians.

## Case Study

Rita is a 55-year-old native Appalachian, who returned home from a visit with relatives and discovered her teen-age daughter, who had died the day before. Her daughter had used a shotgun to take her life, mimicking recent suicides of her uncle and cousin.

Rita's life had been characterized by abandonment. When she was six, her mother died, and she was raised by an uncle and aunt. She was abandoned by her first husband, leaving her with two small children. Two years ago when her second husband died, she experienced another abandonment.

In Rita's networks, suicide was labeled as the coward's way out. Rita had difficulty in believing that her daughter's death was the will of God and that there was no redemption or forgiveness for her daughter, since suicide was a sin in destroying God's holy temple. Troubled by many physical symptoms, she sought care from her physician, who referred her to the area mental health center. She stopped after two visits. The counselor had only asked questions, rather than telling Rita how she could rid herself of her grief and restore her faith in God.

## References

Eller, R. D. (1982). *Miners, millhands, and mountaineers: Industrialization of the Appalachian South, 1880-1930.* Knoxville, TN: University of Tennessee Press.

Keefe, S. E. (1986). Southern Appalachia: Analytical models, social services, and native support systems. *American Journal of Community Psychology, 14,* 479-498.

Keefe, S. E. (1992). Ethnic identity: The domain of perceptions of and attachment to ethnic groups and cultures. *Human Organization, 51,* 35-43.

Mortensen, P. L. (1992). *Literacy and regional difference: Problems with the invention of Appalachia.* Paper presented at the Annual Meeting of the Conference on College Composition and Communication, Cincinnati, OH. (ERIC Document Reproduction Service No. ED 346 428)

Williams, C. (1961). *The southern mountaineer in fact and fiction.* Unpublished doctoral dissertation, New York University, New York.

# CHAMORROS

*Patricia Pier*

### Overview

Chamorros are commonly referred to as Guamanians in the United States. More accurately, the term "Chamorro" is a racial, ethnic, and cultural identification, as well as the language of the indigenous people of the Marianas Islands (Untalan, 1991). Historically, the term Guamanians came into use shortly after World War II when the alliances of the Chamorro people were divided by war. The war and its aftermath resulted in the use of the term Guamanians to distinguish the Chamorros of Guam and those of the Northern Marianas (Shimizu, 1982).

Guam became a possession of the United States in 1898. In 1950, when Guam became a Territory of the United States, the Chamorros were granted U.S. citizenship. It was not until 1975 that the Northern Marianas became a Commonwealth of the United States (Ridgell, 1982).

The Chamorros on Guam, the Northern Marianas, and the continental United States are descendants of a resilient people who have survived near annihilation due to wars, colonization, and disease. Chamorros live throughout the United States and their transition into mainstream American society has posed numerous difficulties which affect the psychological well-being of the Chamorro people.

### Demographics

In the 1990 U.S. Census, Chamorros (referred to as Guamanians) represented the third largest Pacific Island group in the United States not including those living on Guam. Of the 133,000 people living on Guam, over 57,000 claim Chamorro ethnicity (U.S. Census, 1991). Chamorros live in every state in the United States (over 50,000 Guamanians and Northern Marianas islanders) with the largest concentration living in California (Shimizu, 1982). Given these figures,

the total number of Chamorros in the United States, including the Territory of Guam exceeds 107,000. Chamorros have been affected by political changes and efforts to acculturate the people of Guam and the Northern Marianas to American society; however, society's treatment of Chamorros has not been ideal.

### Society's Treatment of Chamorros

Munoz (1978) described Chamorros as invisible minorities. They are frequently mistaken for other minority groups with similar physical characteristics. Because the Chamorro culture, language, and history are generally unknown to most Americans, Chamorros are often treated as foreigners. The absence of ethnic recognition in American society has resulted in unintentional racism and the lack of attention to Chamorros' unique educational, social, psychological, employment, and financial needs.

### Significant Within Group Differences Among Chamorros

Chamorros have coped with tremendous changes over the last one hundred years. Untalan (1991) highlighted the effect of change on the Chamorro people. These changes include high suicide rates among youth, alcoholism, drug abuse, family violence, high crime rates, juvenile delinquency, and a potential loss of language and cultural identity. Changes have also resulted in the breakdown of traditional or extended family relationships.

There are seven salient differences among Chamorros which may be viewed on a continuum. The first difference arises from an individual's identity with the Chamorro culture which may range from a general ethnic identification to the full integration of the Chamorro language, acceptance of beliefs and values, and the perpetuation of the cultural practices. The second difference is the value of interdependence versus independence and individual achievement. The third difference is the importance of the nuclear family versus the extended family. The fourth difference is the importance of familial obligations which include reciprocity and responsibility versus self-reliance. The fifth difference is the respect for the role and importance of women versus viewing women in a subservient position. The sixth difference is respect and a high regard for the elderly versus relegating them to a position of less importance. The seventh difference is the spiritual beliefs in the supernatural, which range from acceptance to designating such beliefs as nonsense.

These differences in behaviors and beliefs of Chamorros represent a variety ranging from those who maintain a "traditional" Chamorro lifestyle to those who have acculturated to American society. Nevertheless, most Chamorros are exposed to or maintain the worldview of the Chamorro culture.

### The Worldview of Chamorros

The extended family system is of paramount importance in Chamorro society. The family maintains prominence within the psychological life of the individual primarily because of its ability to provide emotional, social, physical, and financial support. Therefore, the family's needs and demands have priority over the needs of the individual members. Interdependence, mutuality, and family loyalty are at the core of relationships. Accomplishments of individual family members are recognized by the extended family, as is the shame of transgressions. In addition to the family as a source of strength, the notion of family loyalty may hinder an individual's efforts to seek help. Consequently, Chamorros are concerned about how their behavior will affect the family.

Respect is an integral part of Chamorro society. This respect is extended to the elderly, the family, personal relationships, nature, and "taotaomonas," the spiritual ancestors of the Marianas Islands.

Bringing shame intentionally or unintentionally upon one's self or others is the most profound social violation for Chamorros. Therefore, the task of resolving problems is often dealt with indirectly and circuitously. A confrontive approach is considered primitive and witnessing someone's embarrassment is an affront to both the observer and the subject (Untalan, 1991).

The Catholic Church is central in the private and public life of Chamorros. Cultural traditions and activities revolve around the religious rituals such as fiestas, weddings, and funerals. Religious beliefs have also provided a source of strength and support.

Although Chamorros utilize western medicine, they continue to turn to suruhanos, the traditional healers of the Chamorro people. The suruhano's concept of disease has its origin in the belief that illness is a result of spiritual or natural causes. Their method of curing involves medicinal plants, body lotions, dietary advice, massage, and the inherent curing power of the healer (McMakin, 1978).

### Successful Programs and Implications for Working With Chamorros

There are several factors that enhance a program's level of effectiveness in providing services to Chamorros. Successful programs: (1) recognize the client's identity as an indigenous and distinct ethnic group; (2) understand the effect of acculturation and cultural identity on the psychological well-being of their clients; (3) assess the level of acculturation to determine the role of the family in the diagnosis and treatment of the client; (4) utilize familial support in the helping process and in family therapy when appropriate; (5) explore the spiritual beliefs of the client and are sensitive to their worldview; and (6) understand the psychological stress resulting from in-migrations which may cause a sense of loss of power and control in their lives (Untalan, 1991).

### Accessibility and Availability of Services

Shimizu (1982) and Untalan (1991) described several factors that limit the utilization of mental health services among Chamorros. First, mental health issues are believed to be a sign of weakness, thus risking embarrassment to the individual and the family. Second, the family is likely to take care of and support individuals experiencing problems. Third, many people are unaware that services are available to them. Fourth, some mental health practitioners are insensitive to the Chamorro identity and cultural characteristics. Fifth, there is limited acess to professionals who speak the Chamorro language or who understand the unique cultural issues of Chamorros, thereby limiting therapeutic effectivness and participation in a helpng relationship, training, and research.

## Implications for Practice, Training, and Research

Chamorros are a distinct ethnic group who often feel neglected by American society. Acknowledgement of Chamorro identity is helpful in establishing positive counselor/client relationships and in encouraging Chamorros to participate in practice, training, and research. Moreover, an understanding of Chamorro cultural values which include the importance of respect, the family, issues of shame, and the way of handling confrontation would enhance the development of positive relationships between Chamorros and mental health counselors. The notion of reciprocity is also important. The client or family may give a gift or invite the counselors to social events as a token of appreciation. These gifts or invitations must be dealt with tactfully, for rejection may mark the end of a counseling relationship. If Chamorros are utilized as subjects in research studies, refreshments and time to socialize are viewed as signs of respect and reciprocity. Chamorros also respect researchers who explain the purpose of the study and who later provide information about their findings. Collaborating with Chamorros or individuals who are proficient in the Chamorro language and culture may facilitate the participation of Chamorros and enhance the effectiveness of practice, training, and research.

## Conclusion

Chamorros are a resourceful and resilient people who take pride in their culture and families. In the past, they have survived numerous threats to their existence as a distinct ethnic group. Today, they are coping with the changes as a result of their exposure to differing American values and beliefs. The challenge appears to be that of educating Chamorros of the potential benefits of counseling, as well as educating practitioners to provide a therapeutic relationship that honors Chamorro uniqueness and which will increase counselor understanding and effectiveness.

## Case Study

Martha and Michael, a middle-agd Chamorro couple, live in California with two teenage daughters, Tia and Maria. Martha visited a counselor a year ago regarding her unsatisfactory relationship with her daughter, Tia. Martha characterized Tia's behavior as disrespectful and hostile towards her parents, teachers, and visiting relatives. Martha did not return after the first session because she was ashamed that she had to talk to strangers about a family problem.

Her return to counseling was precipitated because her elderly mother would be living with the family. Martha was fearful that Tia would be disrespectful and make her mother's stay difficult. Martha said she felt very isolated and too embarrassed to talk to her friends or relatives. She felt like a failure and shielded Tia's behavior from her husband because of how he might respond. The counselor recommended that her husband Michael attend the next meeting with their two daughters. In response to Martha's doubt that Tia would come, the counselor suggested that Tia be encouraged to come the first time and not return if she did not want to continue.

The family arrended five sessions.What emerged was that although Tia and her sister shared similar feelings of frustration, Maria would not confront her parents because she did not want to show disrespect. In the sessions, both girls expressed irritation at the steady stream of family members temporarily living in their home, particularly when they were asked to make changes in their schedules and entertain family members they had never met. They were pleased that their grandmother would be living with them, because they knew she had become more fragile and lonely since the death of their grandfather. The sessions resulted in an understanding that Tia and Maria would be involved in discussions about future family visits and Martha and Michael agreed to continue couple's counseling.

### References

McMakin, P. D. (1978). The Suruhanos: Traditional curers on the island of Guam. *Micronesia, 14*(1) 13-67.

Munoz, F. (1978). Pacific Islanders: A perplexed neglected minority. In L. F. Ignacio (Ed.), *Asian Americans and Pacific Islanders* (pp. 283-291). San Jose, CA: Filipino Development Associates.

Ridgell, R. (1982). *Pacific nations and territories: The islands of Micronesia, Melanesia, and Polynesia.* Honolulu, HI: Bess Press.

Shimizu, D. (1982). Mental health needs assessment: The Guamanians in California (Doctoral dissertation, University of Massachusetts, 1982). *Dissertation Abstracts International.* (University Microfilms No. 82-29608).

United States Bureau of the Census (1991). *Current Population Reports, Population Estimates and Projections* (Series No. CB91-215). Washington, DC: Author.

Untalan, F. F. (1991). Chamorros. In N. Makuau (Ed.), *Handbook of social services for Asian and Pacific Islanders* (pp. 171-182). Westport. CT: Greenwood Press.

### Related Words:

Guamanian, Marianas Islands, Saipan, Tinian, and Rota.

# Counseling Chinese Americans

*Frederick T. L. Leong*
*Elayne L. Chou*

### Overview

According to 1990 Census data, Asian Americans make up 2.8% of the United States' population. Chinese Americans are 23.8% of all Asian Americans, making them the largest group of Asian Americans. Specifically, Chinese Americans, numbering 1,645,472, make up 0.7% of the United States population (Barringer, Gardner, & Levin, 1993).

Significant within-group differences feature some Chinese Americans who are well educated and highly acculturated, and others who are poorly educated and more traditional (Sue & Sue, 1991). Chinese Americans are clustered in the technical/ professional fields like engineering or medicine, as well as the unskilled service industries like restaurant workers or garment factory workers. In 1980, median family income for Chinese Americans ($22,600) was slightly higher than the national median ($19,900), but the poverty rate of Chinese Americans (13.5%) was higher than the national average (13%).

### Unique Issues

Historically, Chinese Americans have faced discrimination in the form of immigration exclusion acts. They have been stereotyped as exotic, unassimilable, and immoral. More recently, stereotypes portray them as law-abiding, quiet, intelligent, and hardworking (Gaw, 1982). Gaw suggests that both kinds of stereotypes are harmful because they ignore individual differences and prevent accurate assessment of Chinese Americans' mental health needs.

According to Huang (1991), some social and psychological issues Chinese Americans face have to do with United States society. These include the immigration experience and its stresses (e.g., culture shock, alienation), racism, and discrimination. One could also add to this list anti-immigrant sentiment and harassment. Huang also addresses issues Chinese Americans face with other people. These include familial conflict between generations, which can be compounded by language barriers. Two issues of intense conflict between generations are choice in dating and choice in achievement. Likewise, acculturation conflict can result in feelings of depression, identity conflict, and powerlessness within the individual.

A common issue for Chinese Americans is their acculturation level and ethnic-identity status. Sue and Sue (1971; 1990) describe three ways in which Chinese Americans may adjust to the conflicting demands of Asian and American cultures: "traditionalists" retain traditional values and live up to their families' expectations; "marginal persons" become overwesternized by rejecting traditional Asian values, existing in the margin of the two cultures; and "Asian Americans" formulate a new identity which integrates Asian and American cultures without completely rejecting one or the other.

### Belief System and Worldview

Historically, Chinese conceptions of mental health and mental illness have moved from supernatural beliefs, to an emphasis on natural forces, to a somatic focus on the human body as a source of abnormality. Since the 19th century, psychological causes for mental illness have been accepted, although the preferred method of treatment is still herbs and medicine (Lum, 1982).

Huang (1991) suggests that the traditional Chinese world view revolves around interconnections between mind and body, parent and child, and neighbor and neighbor. While

Westerners value autonomy and independence, Chinese traditionally value harmony, togetherness, and unity. Chinese culture was traditionally a shame-based culture that emphasized public disgrace as punishment, as opposed to the Western guilt-oriented culture's emphasis on self-blame as punishment. The four primary coping strategies in Chinese culture were endurance, looking the other way, not thinking too much, and activity.

Modern Chinese American values still retain some traditional aspects. According to Sue and Sue (1991), these values include: filial piety, stress on family bonds and unity, importance of roles and status, somatization of mental problems, control over strong emotions, stress on academic achievement, and low assertiveness. Huang (1991) pointed out that emotional problems still tend to be expressed in somatic ways. As such, most Chinese Americans do not view "talk therapy" as particularly helpful and they seek therapy only as a last resort.

Finally, Chinese American culture values self-control and the inhibition of strong emotions; individuals learn that their behavior is very significant in that it reflects upon the entire family. If one has feelings that might disrupt family harmony, one is expected to restrain those feelings (Sue & Sue, 1972). Lin (1958; cited in Huang, 1991) comments that the, "Chinese worldview emphasizes the interpersonal to such an extent that the Chinese look to their relationships with people instead of to themselves as the cause of their stress" (p. 86).

### Successful Counseling Programs

Acculturation is a major moderator of the counseling attitudes and experiences of Asian Americans in general, and Chinese Americans in particular (e.g., Sue & Sue, 1972. Leong, 1986. Uba, 1994). High-, middle-, and low-acculturated Chinese Americans require different amounts and types of modifications to Western-oriented mental health services. The following points are important to consider when counseling these three groups of clients.

1. Highly acculturated Chinese Americans are more likely to use traditional Western-based mental health and counseling services, which are available in their communities. Relatively little modifications to Western-oriented counseling approaches are needed in order to be successful with these Chinese Americans.

2. Chinese Americans who exhibit a medium level of acculturation may be willing to use traditional Western-oriented counseling services, but they may hold traditional Chinese values, beliefs, and customs which can interfere with Western-oriented counseling services (see Sue & Sue, 1990). Counselors and therapists need to be flexible and ready to make modifications to their counseling approaches in order to be helpful to them (see Leong, in press).

3. Chinese Americans who exhibit a low level of acculturation are likely to resist counseling from these western-oriented mental health agencies. Two types of alternative programs may be particularly helpful:

   - Owing to the high level of stigma associated with mental health problems for Chinese Americans, Sue & Sue (1990) have suggested that counseling may be offered indirectly by targeting areas that are much more acceptable to Chinese Americans. One of these areas may be academic and vocational counseling. Within the context of academic and vocational counseling services, mental health problems may be addressed in a culturally acceptable manner. Two other areas are occupational attainment and physical health. Workshops that help Chinese Americans advance their occupational aspirations and community-based "health fairs" aimed at improving their physical health can serve as successful programs for helping them with any co-incidental psychological problems.

   - A second alternative is parallel services (Sue, 1977). Asian Americans' mental health needs can be met more effectively by the development and implementation of counseling services which are offered in parallel to the mainstream Western-oriented agencies. These parallel mental health service agencies would feature characteristics that would render services both more culturally relevant and appropriate for Asian Americans. For example, these parallel services would be located directly in the ethnic neighborhoods where the majority of Asian Americans live; such services would feature bicultural and bilingual professionals who could more easily understand and identify with the problems of their clients. Interventions would be modified to fit with the values, customs, and expectations of their clients.

### Mental Health Services and Program Needs

Highly acculturated Chinese Americans are likely to benefit from the mainstream Western-oriented counseling services. However, low-acculturation Chinese Americans need special programs to meet their mental health needs. Mainstream mental health agencies must use more of the indirect-services approach in order to reach more Chinese Americans. In addition, given their success and effectiveness, more parallel agencies are needed in those cities with high concentrations of Chinese Americans.

### Implications for Training and Practice

As mentioned above, it is the medium-acculturation Chinese Americans who are most likely to need modifications of western-oriented counseling approaches. In order to increase actual utilization rates and to minimize premature terminations from counseling among these Chinese Americans, counselors and therapists need to be trained, either in their original training programs or as part of their continuing education, to make these necessary modifications to their western-oriented approaches (see Leong, in press). Modifications would involve integrating cultural values, beliefs, and attitudes of Chinese Americans into actual counseling interventions. For the low-acculturation Chinese Americans, even more drastic modifications may be needed to

Western-oriented counseling services. For some low-acculturation Chinese Americans, counselors may have to discard Western-models altogether and start from scratch. The references at the end of this article provide a resource for identifying and understanding important cultural differences for medium- and low-acculturation Chinese Americans.

### Case Study

In this case study, readers will recognize the issues and problems raised in earlier sections of this chapter.

Mrs. Chung Wai Ching (Chung is the family name) is a first generation 53-year-old Chinese woman who was referred to the community mental health center by her family physician (Dr. Tan). She came to the United States two years ago from China, accompanied by her husband who was studying for a doctorate in engineering at the local university. In the last 12 months, she had presented to her physician with a range of physical symptoms (extreme fatigue, lethargy, headaches, and gastro-intestinal problems) for which Dr. Tan could find no clear pattern or etiology. After several sessions, Dr. Tan finally convinced Mrs. Chung that she might be depressed and that she should see a specialist, i.e., a counselor at the community mental health center. During the first session with the counselor (Dr. Green), Mrs. Chung was quite reticent and only responded to questions with brief replies and no elaboration. Dr. Green found it difficult to engage Mrs. Chung during the session since she spoke only limited English, appeared reluctant to establish eye contact, and was not very "psychologically-minded." With some probing, she did express considerable doubt to Dr. Green as to the value of talking about her personal problems and was surprised at the end of the session that he did not prescribe medication for her physical problems. While she indicated politely to Dr. Green that she would give counseling a try, she did not return for subsequent appointments nor did she return phone calls from the community mental health center. When Dr. Green contacted Dr. Tan about the failure of the referral, he was told by Dr. Tan that Mrs. Chung had found relief from a local herbalist and seemed to be faring much better.

## References

Barringer, H. R., Gardner, R. W., & Levin, M. J. (1993). *Asians and Pacific Islanders in the United States*. New York, NY: Russell Sage Foundation.

Gaw, A. (1982). Chinese Americans. In A. Gaw (Ed.), *Cross-cultural psychiatry* (pp. 1-29). Littleton, MA: PSG Publishing Co.

Huang, K. (1991). Chinese Americans. In N. Moknau. (Ed.), *Handbook of social services for Asian and Pacific Islanders* (pp. 79-96). New York, NY: Greenwood Press.

Leong, F. T. L. (1986). Counseling and psychotherapy with Asian-Americans: Review of the literature. *Journal of Counseling Psychology, 33,* 196-206.

Leong, F.T.L. (in press). Toward an integrative model for cross-cultural counseling and psychotherapy. *Applied and Preventive Psychology.*

Lum, R. C. (1982). Mental health attitudes and opinions of Chinese. In E. E. Jones & S. J. Korchin (Eds.), *Minority mental health* (pp. 165-189). New York, NY: Praeger.

Sue, D. & Sue, D. W. (1991). Counseling strategies for Chinese Americans. In C. C. Lee & B. L. Richardson (Eds.), *Multicultural issues in counseling: New approaches to diversity* (pp. 79-90). Alexandria, VA: American Association for Counseling and Development.

Sue, D. W. & Sue, D. (1990). Counseling Asian Americans. In D. W. Sue & D. Sue (Eds.), *Counseling the culturally different* (2nd ed., pp. 189-208). New York, NY: Wiley.

Sue, D. W. & Sue, S. (1972). Counseling Chinese-Americans. *Personnel and Guidance Journal, 50*(8), 637-644.

Sue, S. (1977). Community mental health services to minority groups: Some optimism, some pessimism. *American Psychologist, 32,* 616-624.

Sue, S. & Sue, D. W. (1971). Chinese-American personality and mental health. *Amerasia Journal, 1,* 36-49.

Uba, L. (1994). *Asian Americans: Personality patterns, identity, and mental health.* New York: Guilford Press.

# Filipino Americans

*Darryl Salvator*

## Overview

Persons of Filipino ancestry collectively rank as the second largest Asian ethnic group living in the United States. The U. S. Bureau of the Census (1990) documents more than 1,406,770 foreign or U. S. born Filipinos residing in the United States as compared to only 501,000 documented foreign or U. S. naturalized Filipino citizens in 1980. Despite landmark numbers of Filipino Americans, there remains a scarcity of information about them and their mental health profile.

The Filipino American experience, in conjunction with the inundation of diverse immigrants to the United States, may operate as a prototype for understanding this and other ethnic groups and increase sensitivity to their mental health needs and issues (Tompar-Tiu & Sustento-Seneriches, 1995). Thus, there exists a definite need for culture-specific descriptions and recommendations for counseling interventions designed towards each ethnic minority group (McDermott, Tseng, & Maretzki, 1980). In order for counselors to properly service the unique needs of this population, they will need to acquire some knowledge of Filipino culture, psychosocial characteristics, cultural needs, and the unique challenges associated with counseling persons from the diverse Filipino background.

## The Philippine-American Connection

The Philippines is a tropical, southeast Asian archipelago of about 7,107 fragmented islands separated into three major land groupings: Luzon (northern group), Visayas (central areas), and Mindanao (southern region). The unique environment holds significant implications for the establishment and maintenance of strong regionalism consistently witnessed in the Philippine setting, with regional traditions and customs proliferated by first generation Filipino Americans (Tompar-Tiu & Sustento-Seneriches, 1995).

Pre-colonial Filipinos had their own distinct cultures and traditions, literature, arts, religion,and social structures which were shaped by their surrounding environment and neighbors. For over three centuries after being "discovered" by Ferdinand Magellan in 1521, the islands became Spain's colony. On June 12, 1896, the first Philippine Republic was instituted following a national revolution against Spanish rule. Despite this, the Philippines were ceded to the United States from Spain and become a U. S. protectorate until 1946, when they finally achieved self determination and nationhood.

Filipino population in the Philippines is comprised of 75 ethnolinguistic groups, speaking over 100 different languages, all of which belong to the larger Austronesian language group. Although Pilipino (Tagalog) has been instituted as the nation's official language, most Filipinos prefer using their regional vernacular. Whereas it is imperative to acknowledge the variances among Filipinos in terms of their regionalism, they also have the tendency to distinguish themselves more as one ethnocultural group when they become immigrants (Anderson, 1983).

## Cultural Beliefs and Values

Filipino culture is derived from and developed through an integrated mixture of Malaysian, Chinese, Indonesian, Spanish, and American influences. This has important significance for the stereotypical characteristics and within-group diversity shared among Filipinos. For example, Malay influence may account for the persistence of animism, fatalism, clannishness, and group affinity; whereas, the Spanish influence is evident in the predominance of Catholicism, in the impact on language, and in the acute respect for and obedience to authority (Ponce, 1980).

The indigenous personality theory, *sikolohiyang Pilipino*, states that shared identity and strong equivalence with one's fellow men is the basic core value of all Filipino values (Enriquez, 1990). Enriquez points out the following traditional values: interaction with others on an equal basis; sensitivity to and regard for others; respect and concern; helping out; understanding and making up for others' limitations; and, rapport and acceptance.

The basic unit of value transactions is the traditional Filipino family. This is the nuclear family, composed of the father-husband, mother-wife, and children, as well as the bilateral extended family, which includes both paternal and maternal relatives. A Filipino's concept of self is heavily influenced by identification with his or her nuclear support of all its members. Interdependence is the norm among all individuals within the family (Tompar-Tiu & Sustento-Seneriches, 1995).

Fathers are responsible for being the principal breadwinner and support for the family. He is the high authority figure and the role of fathering is often defined in terms of discipline. Mothers are mainly responsible for child rearing as well as the social, religious, health, enculturation, and educational activities of the family. Children are considered premier and are found everywhere in social situations. Older siblings (*manong/manang*) are expected to help with parental responsibilities like child rearing and discipline. Affiliation among the children increase a sense of support for one another and ease the burden of familial responsibilities.

In addition, ritual kinship alliances are promulgated through the *compadrazgo system* of extending the family with godparents and marriage sponsors. This system ritually guarantees the synergistic social, emotional, and economic support among the godparents, parents, and godchildren (Tompar-Tiu & Sustento-Seneriches, 1995).

### Cultural Characteristics and Traits Affecting Filipino Behavior

Several cultural characteristics profoundly affecting Filipino behavior include patron-client relationships, personalism, familism, Hiya, Amor Propio, Pakikisama (Smooth Interpersonal Relationships), Bahala Na, and Utang na Loob.

Virtually all relationships in the Philippines are patron-client interactions which help delineate the reciprocal commitments within social hierarchies. Steinberg (1994) states, "The little man or woman know what he or she has to do to remain in favor with the boss, and the patron understands how to protect, support, and sustain the network below." Respect for authority figures is highly valued and subordinates (usually defined in context of the social interactions) are expected not to disagree openly or talk back to them (i.e., elders, parents, lawyers, etc.). Filipinos may regard their priests as God-like and may follow their recommendations but be too embarrassed to question them.

Personalism or the personal quality of Filipino interactions (Jocano, 1981) may explain why they have difficulties separating objective and perfunctory events from their own emotional attachment. Filipinos have the propensity to associate with persons rather than to institutions or agencies. For example, if a college student's midterm essay is critiqued by the professor, the Filipino will often accept the criticism personally— as an attack on their self-esteem. Moreover, Filipino clients will seek out a hospital or agency where they know some employees. This is a significant aspect in relation to mental health services because Filipinos may stop attending the agency that has changed some or most of its employees

From infancy, the importance of honor, loyalty, and family cohesiveness among Filipino kin are enculturated. Family problems are significant stressors that can trigger mental disorders (Tompar-Tiu & Sustento-Seneriches, 1995). Any mental illness suffered by a family member is considered the family illness and may cause embarrassment and dishonor the family unit. It is also commonplace to see a Filipino patient escorted and accompanied by a family member as well as be present while the doctor is attending the client.

Hiya can be translated quickly as "shame" or a

sense of social propriety. A Filipino's behavior is determined by what others will say, think, or do. It is often times inner-directed and presents the Filipino person with a slight discomfort in immediate social situations. Hiya is a form of self-deprecations, involving embarrassment, inferiority, and shyness all arising from improper behavior, and is one of the more powerful sanctions operating to maintain the overall system of social relationships (Ponce, 1980). For example, a Filipino may say, "I lost face because my teacher showed my poor grade to everyone in class" thus eliciting a negative reaction from the embarrassed person.

Amor Propio comes from the Spanish meaning, "love of self." It denotes a good feeling about oneself as well as a sense of individual well-being. The Filipino experiences great sensitivity to any personal insult that results in egotistical injury; specifically the failure to recognize one's social status and family standing. Guthrie (1968) stated the Filipino's "...fragile sense of personal worth leaves him specially vulnerable to negative remarks from others and leads him to be vigilant to signs of status that will indicate how he stands in his group at the moment."

Pakikisama explains group solidarity and doing things together. As a value, it favors the avoidance of direct confrontation that could lead to negative or deviant behaviors. Ponce (1980) claims that intermediate forms of aggression, often expressed by culturally acceptable norms are commonplace (i.e., metaphors or analogies in dialogue, humor, blaming of others, gossip/*tsismis*, etc.).

Bahala Na denotes the quiescent acceptance of one's fate (i.e., hardships, socioeconomic status, role in society, etc.) and the idea that the Filipino has virtually no control over his/her own destiny in life. The essence of this value consists of accepting an unpredictable situation, belief in a higher power (*Bathala*), and determination in the face of uncertainty, which may help the Filipino cope with the ill effects of events beyond their control (Tompar-Tiu & Sustento-Seneriches, 1995).

The psychosocial concept of Utang na Loob refers to the Filipino's debt of gratitude, moral obligation, and reciprocal expectation based upon favors or unsolicited assistance. The Utang na Loob may not have immediate rewards, but if the beneficiary with this trait is still alive—it is expected to last forever—even extending to family and relatives. The failure to repay this moral obligation is considered extremely shameful and disrespectful.

### Case Study

Domingo, a twenty-seven-year-old Filipino male from the rural Ilocos province of the Philippines felt good about his ability to work at an automotive shop and help pitch in to the family finances. Unfortunately, an accident at work which resulted in a broken leg caused him to experience depression. He was referred by the doctor and physical therapist to see a counselor after they suspected that there was something more to his lethargic behavior than a broken fibula.

Domingo became very motivated and cooperative when the counselor offered his help in communicating with his supervisor, doctor, and physical therapist, in relation to his symptoms, emotional/physical handling of his leg injury, and urge at returning to work. He was not feeling good about himself after both the doctor and physical therapist criticized his family's healing methods of prayer, ointment, herbs, and massage. The counselor empathized and acknowledged his client's cultural concepts and explained the therapeutic and diagnostic motives and procedures. Domingo immediately perceived the counselor as a trusted authority figure, who could explain the doctor's and physical therapist's methods to him in an effort to ease his uncertainties and fears. After this, he as able to disclose some depressing feelings and thoughts concerning his injury.

### Implications for Counseling Services

Given the fact that Filipinos are likely to exceed Chinese immigrants to become the largest Asian immigrant group within the next 10 years (Bouvier & Agresta, 1987), there remains a paucity of literature and information in relation to the mental health needs and concerns of Filipino Americans. Even more alarming is that much less is known about how effectively (if at all) Filipino Americans utilize the mental health system and treatment approaches in the United States (Tompar-Tiu & Sustento-Seneriches, 1995).

## References

Anderson, J. N. (1983). Health and illness in Filipino immigrants. *Western Journal of Medicine, 139,* 818-819.

Bouvier, L. F., and Agresta, A. (1987). The future of Asian populations of the United States. In J. T. Fawcett and B. V. Carino (Eds.), *Pacific Bridges: The New Immigration from Asia and the Pacific Islands.* Straten Island, N. Y.: Center for Migration Studies.

Enriquez, V. G. (1990). *Hellside in Paradise: The Honolulu Youth Gangs.* A Report submitted to the Community Affairs Committee, Center for Philippine Studies. Honolulu, HI.: University of Hawaii.

Guthrie, G. M. (1968). *Six perspectives on the Philippines.* Manila: Bookmark.

Jocano, F. L. (1995) Management and Culture: A Normative Approach. In A. Tompar-Tiu & J. Sustento-Seneriches *Depression and other mental health issues: The Filipino American experience.* San Francisco: Jossey-Bass, Inc. Publishers.

McDermott, J. F., Tseng, W., & Maretzki, T. W. (1980). *Peoples and cultures of Hawaii: A psychocultural profile.* Honolulu, HI.: University of Hawaii Press.

Tompar-Tiu, A. & Sustento-Seneriches, J. (1995). *Depression and other mental health issues: The Filipino American experience.* San Francisco: Jossey-Bass, Inc. Publishers.

# The Native Hawaiian (Kanaka Maoli) Client

*Kiaka J.S. Gaughen*
*Dorothy K. Gaughen*

## Overview

The Kanaka Maoli (Native Hawaiians) are the indigenous inhabitants of the Hawaiian Islands. They are the descendants of canoe voyagers who, some 2,000 years ago, settled on a cluster of volcanic islands. The first settlers in the Hawaiian Islands are thought by Western writers to have originated in islands known to Europeans as the Marquesas located in the South Pacific (Blaisdell, 1993).

In 1778 Westerners made their first contact with the Native Hawaiians. At the time of contact it was believed that the Hawaiian population was comprised of between 800,000 and 1 million persons. Today the federal census indicates that there are approximately 156,812 Native Hawaiians residing in the islands with another 99,269 people living on the mainland United States (Marsella, Oliveira, Plummer, & Crabbe 1995).

From the time of contact with foreigners, the psychological and physical well-being of Native Hawaiians seriously deteriorated. Treatment for both the psychological and physical problems by the medical professionals and counseling professionals have failed to make a decent improvement on the situation of the native people. Reasons span from ignorance about Hawaiian culture by these professionals and oppression of the people, to the small number of educated Native Hawaiians to service their own population.

## Unique Problems and/or Stressors Faced by Native Hawaiians

There is an agreement among professionals that the physical, psychological and social realities of Hawaiians place them among the most "at-risk" populations within the state of Hawai'i. Studies suggest that Native Hawaiians are faced with the worst health profile of any group within the United States. Blaisdell (1989) asserted that the forced adaptation of Native Hawaiians to European culture undermined Native Hawaiians' physical health. As a result, Native Hawaiians have the shortest life expectancy and the highest overall death rate of any ethnic group in Hawai'i (Blaisdell, 1989; Marsella et al., 1995).

Native Hawaiians also face many risks to their psychological and social well-being. Marsella, et al. (1995) reported high rates of substance abuse, child abuse, depression and suicide among Native Hawaiians. Native Hawaiians are also over represented in the lower economic segments of the state's population as well as in the state's prison system (Marsella et al., 1995).

Native Hawaiians today occupy both poles of the economic and social status spectrum. While there is a growing number of wealthy and influential professional and business leaders of Native Hawaiian ancestry, the vast majority of Native Hawaiians continue to languish at the lower end of the social strata, handicapped by centuries of exploitation, abuse, and racism (Marsella et al., 1995).

Recent assessments of Native Hawaiian children found that they were among the most "at risk" for negative academic outcomes (Native Hawaiian Educational Assessment Project, 1993). This is a major concern because this factor may affect these individuals for the rest of their life, and will have a major impact on the continued existence of Native Hawaiians as a distinct cultural group.

## Significant Within-Group Differences

According to Atkinson, Morten, and Sue(1993), minority people who struggle to understand themselves in terms of their own culture within the dominant culture, a culture which is a subset of the dominant culture, are described by a five-stage Minority Identity Development (MID) model. The five stages for Native Hawaiians are as following:

1. Conformity—the individual is self-depreciating and prefers to be identified with dominant cultural values;
2. Dissonance—the individual develops conflicts about the dominant system and is in a state of cultural confusion;
3. Resistance and Immersion—the individual is more self-appreciating and rejects the dominant society;
4. Introspection—the individual carefully evaluates his or her attitude toward self and the dominant society;
5. Synergistic—the individual accepts his or her cultural identity and develops selective appreciations of the dominant culture.

Many Native Hawaiians are currently moving from the Dissonance stage to the Resistance and Immersion stages. This is a result of a series of Hawaiian renaissance and sovereignty events culminating with one particular historical event in January 1993. It was on this occasion that thousands of Native Hawaiians observed the 100th year of the illegal overthrow of the Hawaiian Nation—the first time that thousands of Native Hawaiians participated in any political function since 1893.

## Belief System and World View
### LOKAHI

According to Marsella, et al.(1995) Native Hawaiians employ a holistic belief system. They perceive everything to be one (*lokahi*). This includes the person (k naka), family ('ohana), nature ('aina), and spiritual world (akua). Native Hawaiians seek to find a sense of balance (pono) with all of these things.

### 'OHANA

In ancient Hawai'i, the family ('Ohana) was the center of all relationships. The 'ohana included members of the extended family and provided each individual a source of warmth, support, and guidance. Family unity, loyalty, and love gave each individual a sense of security and well-being. It was within the 'ohana that children learned their roles, their relationship to the gods and nature, and their place in society.

## A Current Successful Program

Ho'omau Ke Ola, a substance abuse program in Waianae on the island of Oahu, has been successful with Native Hawaiians. The main reason for this is that the program uses the *Lokahi* and *'Ohana* values in its treatment. First, it uses a family and group therapy approach with a focus on Hawaiian culture. This allows the *'Ohana* values to provide a comfortable environment with culturally-relevant support. After this is obtained the next step is to utilize a traditional Hawaiian therapy called *ho'opono'pono* (to correct), a kind of family and group therapy which emphasizes bringing back *lokahi* into the individuals life.

According to Marsella, et al. (1995) *ho'opono'pono* is achieved through discussion, prayer, and forgiveness and is usually led by an elder (*kupuna*) or healer (*kahuna*), who directs the person and family members to tell the truth in a group process format.

## Implications for Counselors

There are basically four implications for counselors. First, they should gain a more comprehensive awareness of what the Hawaiian people have been experiencing throughout history. This will allow counselors to understand the point of view of these unique individuals. Secondly, professionals may want to implement family and group therapy that use traditional Hawaiian therapies and values, such as *Ho'opono'pono*, *'Ohana*, and *Lokahi*. The third suggestion is that counselors need to gain a better understanding of within group differences and also respect individuals who are at different stages of the MID model. Finally there should be more research on Hawaiians and more specifically in the area of Native Hawaiian ethnic identity.

## Case Study

A Native Hawaiian woman kept seeing visions of her dead grandmother. The sighting always occurred when there was some sort of crisis in this woman's life. This went on for a few weeks when the woman's health began to decline. In conversation with her sister, this woman told her sister what she has been experiencing. The sister suggested that she seek advice from a family advisor, in this case an old Hawaiian aunt.

The woman's aunt said the visions occurred because the grandmother was unhappy with something in this woman's life. The aunt asked her if there was any reason the grandmother could be unhappy. The woman said that she and her husband were having marital problems. So the aunt suggested that she resolve her problems with her husband. She resolved the marital conflict, but the visits from the grandmother continued. She sought advice from the aunt again. The aunt inquired further if there was any other reason for the grandmother to be unhappy. The woman remembered that when she had her third child, she had a dream of her grandmother. In her dream the grandmother told her to give the child a specific name. However when the child was born the husband did not want the child to have the name the mother received in her dream. It is customary for a child to be given a name by a relative, even if it is received in a dream.

Finally the aunt told the woman to take the child to the grave of the grandmother and to apologize. When the woman did this the visits from the grandmother ceased. This case study is an example of bringing the *lokahi* back into the individual's life. It also made use of a cultural ritual as a form of therapy.

## References

Atkinson, D. R., Morten, G., & Sue, D. W. (1993). *Counseling American minorities: A cross cultural perspective* (4th ed.). Dubuque, IA: W.C. Brown.

Blaisdell, K. (1989). Historical and cultural aspects of Native Hawaiian health. *Social Process in Hawai'i, 32* (1), 1-21.

Blaisdell, K. (1993). The health status of the indigenous Hawaiians. *Asian American and Pacific Islander Journal of Health, 1,* 116-160.

Kamehameha Schools Bishop Estate (1993). *Native Hawaiian Educational Assessment Project.* Honolulu: Kamehameha Schools Bishop Estate.

Marsella, A. J.,Olivera, J. M., Plummer, C. M., & Crabbe, K. M. (1995). Native Hawaiian (Kanaka Maoli) culture, mind, and well being. In H. I. McCubbin, E. A. Thompson, A. I. Thompson & J. E. Fromer (Eds.). *Resiliency in ethnic minority families: Native and immigrant American families.* (pp. 93-113). Madison, WI: University of Wisconsin System.

Trask, H. K. (1995). Native sovereignty: A strategy for Hawaiian family survival. In H. I. McCubbin, E. A. Thompson, A. I. Thompson & J. E. Fromer (Eds.). *Resiliency in ethnic minority families: Native and immigrant American Families.* (pp. 133-139) Madison, WI: University of Wisconsin System.

# Critical Demographic and Cultural Considerations for the Education and Counseling of Hispanics

*Gerardo M. Gonzalez*

### Overview

In the United States, the word Hispanic refers to an extremely diverse group of people. The United States Census of the Population classifies Hispanics as Mexican-Origin, Mainland Puerto Rican (those who live in the United States mainland as opposed to the island of Puerto Rico), Cuban-Origin, Central and South American, and Other. However, within these groups there are great differences in history, nationality, immigration patterns, legal status, demographics as well as other important population characteristics. For example, the Mexican-origin population, which accounts for over 60% of the Hispanic population in the United States, calls themselves by various ethnic labels such as Chicano, Mexican American, Mexican, Mexicano, Hispano, Hispanic and Latino. Each of these labels has important connotations based on generational, regional, and political differences. Many Mexican-origin people, whose ancestors date back before the United States' conquest of the Mexican North identify themselves as a Hispano ethnic group rather than as Mexican. This group identifies more closely with their American Indian and Spanish ancestry. Another group of Mexican-origin people who do not label themselves as Mexicans are the Mexican Americans who became part of the middle class during the 1920s, as well as many of the GI families of the 1940s. Pressure brought by outside oppression forced many of these groups, particularly in earlier decades, to hide their Mexican origins under the euphemisms "Spanish" or "Latin American." These individuals led their children to call themselves Americans or Latins in an effort to disassociate themselves from Mexico and its economic problems (Valencia & Menchaca, 1993).

In contrast, since the 1960s, many Mexican-origin groups have shifted back to using labels stressing their Mexican ancestry. This is particularly true of the United States born urban Chicano. In general, the current use of the term Mexican, Mexican American, Mexicano, and Chicano indicates that there is a strong sense of pride in identifying with Mexican culture.

Similarly, there are significant within-group differences among the other United States Hispanic groups. For example, most of the Cuban-origin population in the United States arrived in successive immigration waves following Castro's revolution and takeover of power in Cuba in 1959. However, Cuban migrations to the United States predate this century. By the late 1800s about 100,000 Cubans were concentrated mainly in New York City, Tampa, Key West, and other Florida cities. Fleeing the Cuban wars of independence (1868 to 1895), this first massive wave of immigrants established the tobacco industry in South Florida and largely remained there to become the first large enclave of Cuban-Americans. These early Cuban-Americans and the more recent "Cuban Flotilla" arrivals have very different political orientations, cultural traditions, and language experiences.

These examples of intra-group differences among the Mexican-origin and Cuban-origin population serve to illustrate the risk of overgeneralization when dealing with the "Hispanic" population in the United States. Not only are Hispanics highly diverse in terms of national and geographic origins of the various groups that make up the Hispanic population in the United States, but there are also significant differences within these groups. Therefore, discussions about approaches for counseling and intervention with Hispanics must be tempered by the awareness that broad generalizations are not possible. This limitation not withstanding, it is important to know as much as possible about the Hispanic population in order to design effective interventions.

### Demographic Characteristics

As mentioned above, the United States Census of the Population classifies Hispanics according to whether they are Mexican Americans, Mainland Puerto Ricans, Central and South Americans, Cuban Americans, or Other Hispanics. These four groups comprise what is generally referred to as the "Hispanic" or, more recently, "Latino" population in the United States. By far, the largest of these groups is the Mexican American segment. Mexican Americans make up 62.9% of the Latino population in the United States. The second largest group is Mainland Puerto Ricans, who comprise 12.4% of the Latino population. Following closely in numbers are those of Central and South American descent who make up 11.3% of all United States Latinos. The last two groups, Other Hispanics, which includes persons with roots directly to Spain, and Cuban Americans, constitute 7.9% and 5.3%, respectively of all United States Latinos. All together, the 1990 Census recorded over 22 million Hispanic/Latinos, in the United States. It is projected that by the year 2000, approximately 35 million Hispanics will live in the United States. Hispanics are expected to outnumber African-Americans by the year 2010 (Nicolau & Santiestevan, 1990).

Hispanics are highly concentrated in specific areas of the country. Over three-quarters of all U.S. Hispanics reside in five states, led by California's 35.8% of the total, followed by Texas with 21.1%, New York with 9.8%, and Florida and Illinois with 6.7% and 4.3% respectively. In other words, over half of all Hispanics reside in California and Texas. Moreover, Hispanics are mostly urbanites. The Los Angeles metro area accounts for approximately a third of all Hispanics living in the United States. The next two highest areas of concentration are New York and Miami. Approximately 68% of Hispanics are located in the Los Angeles, New York, Miami, San Francisco, Chicago, and Houston areas. Although Hispanics are likewise rapidly expanding into areas not known for significant concentrations of Hispanics, most of the population growth is expected to take place in the traditional Hispanic areas. Los Angeles and New York will continue to be the two largest Hispanic markets.

The most significant characteristic of Hispanics as a U.S. population group is growth. Between 1980 and 1990 the Hispanic population in the United States grew by about 55%, a rate of growth that far exceeds the growth of any other U.S. racial or ethnic group. This rapid growth is attributable to the group's high fertility rate and the continued immigration of young Hispanics. Only 31.2% of all non-Hispanics are 20 years old and under, compared with 42.2% of Hispanics. While 21.6% of non-Hispanics are 55 and older, only 10.6% of Hispanics are in that age group. The group's median age is 25.5 years, while the median age for non-Hispanics is 32.9 years. Because Hispanics have a greater percentage of their population in the prime child-bearing age classifications, a continuation of their rapid growth rate is assured for the near future.

### Major Problems

Hispanics have a disproportionately high number of families living in poverty. In 1988, the Census Bureau projected that 25.8% of the nation's Hispanic families were living below poverty levels. This rate is more than two and a half times greater than the non-Hispanic rate. Moreover, while the non-Hispanic family poverty rate has slowly but steadily declined, the Hispanic rate has continued to rise (Nicolau & Santiestevan, 1990). In part, this increase in the income gap can be explained by the larger proportion of young Hispanic adults who are just entering the job market. At the same time, because large numbers of Hispanic immigrants have entered the United States in the last several years, the gap also reflects their adjustment, education, and skill levels.

One of the greatest problems for the socioeconomic advancement of Hispanics is the educational achievement of Hispanic youth. The educational system of the United States has not served Hispanic students well. Hispanics have historically been the most undereducated major population group in the United States. Compared to African Americans and Whites, Hispanics have the lowest levels of educational attainment, highest dropout rates, and highest illiteracy rates (Perez & De La Rosa Salazar, 1993). Only one in two Hispanic adults over the age of 25 completed high school. This percentage compares quite unfavorably with the 80% high school completion rate for non-Hispanics. For college completion, only 9% of Hispanics over 25 years of age had attained four years of college. This compares with a 22% college completion rate for non-Hispanics. Such low levels of educational attainment are in large part due to the high levels of school dropout rates among Hispanics. According to the National Center for Educational Statistics, 32.4% of Hispanics 16-24 years old were dropouts in 1990, compared to 13.2% of African-Americans, and only 9.0% of Whites.

Perez and De La Rosa Salazar (1993) attributed both the low educational status of Hispanics and the quality of education they receive to several interrelated factors including poverty; over representation in poor, inner-city, overcrowded, and segregated schools; enrollment below grade level; tracking in nonacademic courses; and limited contact with Hispanic and/or bilingual teachers. For example, Hispanics have the distinction of being the most segregated ethnic/racial group in American schools. Moreover, Chapa and Valencia (1993) projected that Hispanics will attend even more segregated schools in the future and that the deleterious outcomes of attending such schools—especially low achievement, high dropout rates, and inferior college preparation—are likely to intensify. Thus, major changes in educational policy are needed if Hispanics are to be helped out of the cycle of poverty and continued under achievement in education. Without such changes, the rapidly growing number of Hispanic youth will soon become an underclass of unprecedented proportions in America.

## Counseling Interventions

Educational success is the single most important factor in helping Hispanics improve their quality of life in the United States. High rates of inner-city crime, gang violence, drug abuse, unemployment, teenage pregnancy, and sexually transmitted diseases are related to high rates of poverty among the Hispanic population. In turn, high rates of poverty are intimately related to educational attainment. Therefore, long-term interventions designed to reduce the incidence of these problems should focus on creating an environment that makes it possible for individual Hispanic youth to succeed in school. Such interventions, however, must be multifaceted and culturally sensitive. Interventions designed to motivate individuals as well as provide them with the skills and support networks needed for educational success are needed. Unfortunately, in the current school reform climate of higher academic standards and reduced resources, Hispanics are not likely to fare well. In raising academic standards without providing the resources for appropriate developmental and family support, schools are likely to alienate further that student subpopulation we often call "at risk." Hispanic and other minority populations are more likely than Whites to possess one or more of the characteristics or situations associated with being at risk for school failure. Some of these predictors include living with a single parent, having repeated a grade, having a disadvantaged socioeconomic background, being limited in English proficiency, having disciplinary problems at school, having low levels of academic performance as measured by grades, and having irregular attendance patterns (Reyes & Valencia, 1993).

Counselors and other human service professionals should be aware of these potentially conflicting pressures and become advocates for systemic reform that takes into consideration the special needs of Hispanics. Effective advocacy, however, will require the formation of therapeutic alliances between the client, his or her community, and the counselor. Kaune-Wilde (1993) has identified 10 principles, proposed in the literature, for working effectively with Hispanic clients and their communities. These principles include having an understanding of:

1. the family system, which is a very strong source of support and identity for Hispanics;
2. gender roles that are rather rigid and clearly defined, with the man as the authority figure and the woman as the nurturing, loving person who attempts to meet family needs;
3. the role of personalism, the preference for close personal contact between Hispanics;
4. a time orientation that is decidedly here and now;
5. a concept of well-being that refers to both psychological and physical aspects;
6. locus of control, with many Hispanics having an external locus of control because of environmental conditions;
7. the importance of respect, which is present in all interactions, especially when dealing with older persons;
8. the role of confianza (trust) and mutual respect as a cultural bond for relationships among Hispanics;
9. religion as a very important source of support among Hispanics; and
10. language and dialects which have different roots and meaning.

Counselors also need to be aware of the role of acculturation. Acculturation refers to the process of adjustment: the borrowing, acquiring, and adopting of cultural traits from a host society by people who have migrated from another society. Baron (1991) conceptualized the process of acculturation as a multidimensional and multidirectional process whereby immigrant groups incorporate both overt and covert cultural characteristics of the dominant culture. According to Baron, overt cultural characteristics such as dress, language usage, eating habits, and celebrations are more easily incorporated into a new set of patterns and can be more easily observed than covert characteristics such as beliefs, attitudes, values and feelings. Moreover, several personal, social, and demographic variables affect the rate at which acculturation occurs. For example, the personal motivation for

assimilating into the dominant culture, the degree of contact with other groups, and age, all affect acculturation rates. In general, younger persons acculturate more rapidly than older ones. Because youngsters tend to acculturate more rapidly than their parents, this process often exacerbates intergenerational differences. Families who experience the greatest distress are those in which the levels of acculturation within the family unit are most discrepant. Given these findings, it is clear that understanding the concept of acculturation is central to counseling and developing networks among migrant groups in general and Hispanic groups in particular.

**Conclusion**

Hispanics in the United States are a highly diverse population. In addition to significant differences among the various groups that make up what is known as Hispanics or Latinos in the United States, significant within-group differences are also present. In general, however, Hispanics in the United States are a rapidly growing, youthful population. They are highly concentrated in urban centers within a relatively small number of states. As a group, Hispanics have higher rates of poverty than the general population and the gap is growing. As a result, Hispanics experience a disproportionally high incidence of psychosocial problems, such as drug abuse, sexually transmitted diseases, violence, and other social pathologies. At the root of these problems is the lack of educational attainment among Hispanics. Counselors and other human service providers concerned about finding long-term solutions to Hispanic problems should become aware of cultural dynamics that are operative in the Hispanic community. An understanding of such dynamics is important for developing therapeutic alliances needed for effective intervention and advocacy with Hispanic groups. Counselors should become aware of these dynamics and intervene systematically to effect individual and environmental changes that will lead to improvement in the social condition affecting Hispanics in the United States. Otherwise, the evolution of a rapidly growing, youthful Hispanic underclass will become one of the greatest challenges confronting the country in the 21st Century.

## References

Baron, A. (1991). Counseling Chicano college students. In C. C. Lee and B. L. Richardson (Eds.), *Multicultural issues in counseling: New approaches to diversity* (pp. 171-184). Alexandria, VA: American Association for Counseling and Development.

Chapa, J., & Valencia, R. R. (1993). Latino population growth, demographic characteristics, and educational stagnation: An examination of recent trends. *Hispanic Journal of Behavioral Sciences, 15*, 165-187.

Kaune-Wilde, V. (1993). Providing culturally sensitive human development services for Latin Americans. In G. M. Gonzalez, I. Alvarado, & A. S. Segrera (Eds.), *Challenges of cultural and racial diversity to counseling: Mexico City conference proceedings* (pp. 36-43). Alexandria, VA: American Counseling Association.

Nicolau, S., & Santiestevan, S. (Eds.). (1990). *The Hispanic almanac: Edition two.* New York: Hispanic Policy Development Project, Inc.

Perez, S. M., & De La Rosa Salazar, D. (1993). Economic, labor force, and social implications of Latino educational and population trends. *Hispanic Journal of Behavioral Sciences, 15*, 188-229.

Reyes, P., & Valencia, R. R. (1993). Educational policy and the growing Latino student population: Problems and prospects. *Hispanic Journal of Behavioral Sciences, 15*, 258-283.

Valencia, R. R., & Menchaca, M. (1993). Demographic overview of Latino and Mexican-origin populations in the United States: Counseling implications. In G. M. Gonzalez, I. Alvarado, & A. S. Segrera (Eds.), *Challenges of cultural and racial diversity to counseling: Mexico City conference proceedings* (pp. 27-35). Alexandria, VA: American Counseling Association.

# Counseling Japanese Americans

*Mary A. Fukuyama*

## Overview

Japanese Americans constitute the third largest group of Asian/Pacific Americans, with a population estimate of 866,160 (U.S. Bureau of Census, 1990). According to the census bureau, Japanese Americans' mean and median household incomes were 20-25% higher than the average for Asian/Pacific Americans, and only 3.4% of Japanese American families were living below poverty level. The earliest immigrants from Japan arrived around the turn of the 20th century and Japanese American history can be traced through five generations: Issei, Nisei, Sansei, Yonsei, Gosei. The largest concentrations of Japanese Americans can be found in Hawaii and the West Coast of the United States. As a population, Japanese Americans have a slow growth rate in the U.S. The low growth rate can be accounted for by two factors: about two-thirds of all Japanese Americans are native born in the U.S. and have small families, and secondly, immigration from Japan is low. Fewer than 4000 Japanese emigrate to the U.S. annually, as there are few economic incentives to leave Japan (Trueba, Cheng, & Ima, 1993).

## World War II Internment

The most unique social stressor on Japanese Americans was their internment during World War II. West Coast Japanese Americans, numbering around 120,00 (two-thirds of whom were U.S. citizens), were forced to leave their homes and were incarcerated in prison camps for two to three years following U.S. entry into the war against Japan. While military necessity was used as the reason, government sponsored hearings conducted in the 1980's subsequently found that there was no evidence to support these actions.

The internment was traumatic for those incarcerated and also has had an impact on their surviving off-spring (Nagata, 1991).

## Generational Differences

Each generation of Japanese Americans has unique characteristics which are based upon historic and social influences. The original immigrants (called Issei for first generation) were subject to discrimination, racial prejudice, adjustments to a new culture, and language barriers. Economic necessity and white-imposed segregation forced many to live in Japanese communities. Some marriages were arranged by families and some women came to the United States as "picture brides," having never before met their future husbands. This older generation of Japanese Americans may have closer ties to traditional Japanese culture and may have limited English-speaking ability.

The Nisei generation (literally second generation, but first born in the United States) was subject to incredible assimilational forces during World War II. This generation had to prove that it was "200%" American because of the internment camp experience. Nisei men were drafted into a special Army unit known as the "442nd Infantry" and they received many medals for their courage in fighting in Europe. Nisei parents encouraged their children (Sansei) to become educated and successful. Rather than view Sansei as totally acculturated into mainstream America, a more accurate description would be that many Sansei are bicultural or multicultural, having been influenced both by their Japanese cultural heritage and by growing up in the American culture (see Locke, 1992). The younger generations of Japanese Americans (Yonsei, Gosei) may be considered to be even more acculturated, although this would certainly be influenced by the extent of the family involvement in the Japanese American community and by geographic location (e.g.,Hawaii).

Another social variable among Japanese Americans is the outmarriage rate (marrying a partner who is not Japanese American) and mixed-race children. Demographic trends indicate that Japanese Americans have a high rate of outmarriage when compared to other Asian American groups (Mass, 1992). Some of these marriages resulted from "war brides," that is, Japanese women marrying American soldiers after World War II. Others may be indicative of assimilation and breakdown of ethnic boundaries. The impact of intermarriage on the Japanese American community is a complex issue. Mass (1992) recommended that Japanese American communities adopt an inclusive attitude (similar to Hawaii) where individuals are affirmed for both cultural heritages.

A severe stressor on all Japanese Americans, regardless of age, is prejudice and anti-Asian racism. During times of economic recession in the United States, Asians become scapegoats. "Japan-bashing" rhetoric has led to increased physical violence against Asians in the U.S.

## Belief System and World View

The extent to which Japanese Americans are assimilated will affect the degree to which they hold traditional Japanese values. Kitano (1989) has described a model for determining levels of assimilation and ethnic identity to assist counselors in their approach to counseling. Marsella (1993) has outlined several important values from Japanese culture which influence the counseling process: hierarchical status in relationships, collective group identity, tradition and respect for the past, duty and obligation, tolerance for suffering, harmony in relations and in nature, cooperation and competition, and integration of mind-body.

## Implications for Counseling: Training and Practice

Generally, Japanese Americans along with other Asian Americans tend to underutilize mental health services. Mental problems are stigmatized, and the concept of "talk therapy" is unfamiliar. Sue and Zane (1986) recommended that therapists establish credibility through "gift-giving," that is, providing some immediate relief and/or demonstrating the benefits of counseling to the client during the first session. In addition, they recommend that training programs include cultural knowledge of Asian Americans, appreciation of within-group differences, and direct experience with Asian Americans.

Specific counseling stategies to address the traumatic effects of WWII internment on survivors have been developed (Nagata, 1991; Tomine, 1991). Counseling strategies for older Japanese Americans may include techniques adapted from therapies which originated in Japan, such as Morita or Naikan therapy (Itai & McRae, 1994). Although many diverse factors can influence the course of therapy, generally speaking, an approach that emphasizes short-term, goal-oriented treatment, with the therapist taking an active role, may be most effective (Kitano, 1989). Furthermore, the therapist may need to educate the client on the usefulness of therapy, as well as clarify expectations.

## Case Study

A 34-year-old Sansei woman comes to therapy for symptoms of depression. She is concerned about her aging parents, and also feels frustrated with her career development. She has worked loyally as an accountant for one firm, and now feels restricted in terms of advancement. She wonders if the "glass ceiling" is a factor in her being passed over for promotions. Both of her parents were interned during WWII as children, but they have never spoken about their experiences. She is reluctant to reveal her family background, because of feelings of shame. She feels weak for not being able to get over feelings of depression on her own. She has lived a fairly conventional lifestyle, and now feels pressure to have children. Her Japanese American Sansei husband refuses to come to therapy.

This case study includes both personal and social issues which affect Japanese Americans. The therapist will need to consider numerous factors to establish a working alliance.

## References

Itai, G., & McRae, C. (1994). Counseling older Japanese American clients: An overview and observations. *Journal of Counseling and Development, 72,* 373-377.

Kitano, H. H. L. (1989). A model for counseling Asian Americans. In P. B. Pedersen, J. G. Draguns, W. J. Lonner, & J. E. Trimble (Eds.), *Counseling across cultures* (3rd ed., pp. 139-151). Honolulu: University of Hawaii Press.

Locke, D. L. (1992). *Increasing multicultural understanding: A comprehensive model.* Newbury Park: Sage Publications. (ERIC Document Reproduction Service No. ED 350 378)

Marsella, A. J. (1993). Counseling and psychotherapy with Japanese Americans: Cross-cultural considerations. *American Journal of Orthopsychiatry, 63,* 200-208.

Mass, A. I. (1992). Interracial Japanese Americans: The best of both worlds or the end of the Japanese American community? In M. P. P. Root (Ed.), *Racially mixed people in America* (pp. 265-279). Newbury Park: Sage Publications.

Nagata, D. K. (1991). Transgenerational impact of the Japanese American internment: Clinical issues in working with children of former internees. *Psychotherapy, 28,* 121-128.

Sue, S. & Zane, N. (1986). Therapists' credibility and giving: Implications for practice and training in Asian American communities. In M. R. Miranda & H. H. L. Kitano (Eds.), *Mental health research and practice in minority communities: Development of culturally sensitive training programs* (pp. 157-175). Rockville, MD: National Institute of Mental Health.

Tomine, S. I. (1991). Counseling Japanese Americans: From internment to reparation. In C. C. Lee & B. L. Richardson (Eds.), *Multicultural issues in counseling: New approaches to diversity* (pp. 91-105). Alexandria, VA: American Association for Counseling and Development.

Trueba, H. T., Cheng, L., & Ima, K. (1993). *Myth or reality: Adaptive strategies of Asian Americans in California.* Washington, D. C.: The Falmer Press.

# THE KOREAN AMERICANS

*Bryan Soo Kyung Kim*

### Overview

While Korean Americans have been represented among the various ethnic groups in the United States since 1903, the passage of the Immigration Reform Act of 1965 resulted in a recent dramatic increase in their number. In comparison to the initial 11,000 arrivals in 1903, there are currently more than 837,000 Korean American living in the U.S., most of them arriving during the past decade (U.S. Bureau of Census, 1990). At the present, Korean Americans represent one of the largest groups of Asian Americans.

While the reason for immigration may vary with each individual, a majority of recent Korean American arrivals came to the United States either due to a marriage to a U.S. military servicemen, to obtain better economic opportunities, to gain political freedom, or to provide greater educational opportunities for their children. Furthermore, all of them came with the purpose of permanently residing in the U.S.

This paper presents the risk factors, relevant historical information, important cultural values and beliefs, psychological characteristics, and implications to mental health professionals regarding the recently emigrated Korean Americans.

### Risk Factors and Difficulties Experienced

The cultural differences and the language barrier are sources of psychological distress for newly arrived Korean Americans. Korean American men often suffer from underemployment mainly due to the language barrier. While many come to the United States with both a college degree from Korea and professional skills, they tend to settle for a job that requires few skills with little earning potential. Having been the main bread winner in

Korea, they may have difficulty coping with the damaging effects on the ego, as well as adjusting to the loss of social status. The lack of available support that was traditionally offered by an all-male social network in Korea may further exacerbate the difficulties.

Korean American women also face many difficulties. They are forced to take on responsibilities generally not required of them in Korea and are expected to take care of household chores as dictated by Korean culture. Many are often forced to obtain a job to supplement the husband's earnings. For those women who immigrated because of marriages to military servicemen, they often find the melding of two cultures difficult.

Korean American children are caught in a cultural double-bind. While trying to assimilate into the U.S. culture, they are expected to hold onto the Korean culture. Their lack of English proficiency also causes them difficulties in the schools.

While Korean Americans do emigrate with expectations of adjustment problems, they still find it difficult to cope with the accompanying stresses. Consequently, there is a need to offer mental health services to this group of people.

### History

Due to its strategic location between the Asian continent and Japan, the Korean peninsula served as the battleground for numerous conflicts and its people suffered from oppression by other nations (Locke, 1992). At different points in its history, Korea was invaded by Japan, China, and Russia, which propelled Korea to become the "Hermit Kingdom." In 1910, Japan overthrew Korea's monarchy and gained control over the entire peninsula. Soon after regaining its independence in 1945 at the end of World War II,

Korea became divided into North and South with the former allying itself with the SovietUnion and China, and the latter associating itself with the United States. As a result, Korea continues to be a pawn in the power struggle between world powers.

### Cultural Values and Beliefs

Historical events heavily influenced the cultural values and beliefs of all Koreans, including the recently emigrated Korean Americans. One result of these events is that they emphasize independence and autonomy over identity as a distinct group of people. This belief can be seen in their achievement-oriented values. Another result is their strongly held Chinese-influenced, family oriented values.

### Family

Hierarchical relationships, which have roots in Confucianism and are primarily determined by age, play a key role in Korean families (Korean Overseas Information Service, 1990). These families follow strict Confucian patriarchal traditions where the father is the center of the household. He makes most of the decisions affecting the family and everyone is expected to follow them. The father is also expected to uphold the family honor by demonstrating appropriate behavior. Lee and Lee (1990) characterized the relationship between a child and parents into three age-dependent stages. The stages are described as:

1. a period of affection,
2. a period of discipline and education, and
3. a period of dutifulness.

The relationships generally change from infancy into adulthood.

The infant is given much affection which is gradually replaced by discipline and education during the person's adolescent years. This is then replaced by a period of dutifulness when the person begins to care for his/her parents.

During the discipline and education period, Korean children are taught strict rules that guide their relationships with elders (Lee & Lee, 1990). The foremost rule is to demonstrate respect to their elders by using honorific language. Korean children are also taught to obey and listen to their parents and older siblings. In addition, these children are expected to avoid questioning authority figures and are taught to follow the directions of such persons.

### Education

Educational achievement is highly valued in the Korean culture (Korean Overseas Information Service, 1990). The Korean parents' most common reason for immigration to the United States is to provide educational opportunities for their children. This value placed on education has also forced these parents to put intense pressure on their children—failure in school brings shame to the family. While many Korean American students do succeed in school, others do not. Consequently, they often suffer from achievement anxiety (Lee & Cynn, 1991).

### Treatment of Psychological Difficulties Among Korean Americans

Korean Americans generally continue to care for those family members who are psychologically distressed (Harvey & Chung, 1980). However, they tend to regard these individuals as sources of extreme shame for their families, mainly because the difficulties are attributed to a displeasure by ancestral spirits which results in spirit intrusions. The concepts of "palcha," or destiny, and "chaesu," or fortune, are used to explain these supernatural causes.

Korean Americans also believe that psychological difficulties are associated with disharmonious interpersonal relationships. In each "ingan," (the emotional connectedness between persons), and "chong," (the effect of human life), is the central governing substance. For example, Korean Americans tend to express their emotions, both positive or negative, with those whom they feel intimately connected to. The level of intimacy is determined by "nunchi," or the ability to detect and interpret subtle shifts and nuances in interpersonal relations. When the emotional connectedness is disturbed due to a negative "chong," psychological difficulties are created. Restoration of "ingan" through honest communication via direct contact, or through a third person mediator, is possible.

## Case Study

A teacher notices that John, a Korean American adolescent, has begun to falter in his studies. The teacher also notices that John has been involved in acting out and seems to be suffering from depression. The teacher makes inquiries about these observations, but is unsuccessful in gaining information from John. He does not want to talk about them. The teacher then approaches John's best friend who informs her that John has been having difficulties with his parents. The teacher then refers Jonn to a mental health professional.

While risking the embarrassment that he may bring to his family, John, with encouragement from his best friend, begins to share his story with the counselor. John emigrated from Korea seven years ago with his parents. While he has learned the language and has begun to assimilate into the culture, his parents have continued to hold onto Korean cultural values. One of the difficulties experienced by John are the conflicting emotions arising from what he has been exposed to in school in comparison to what his parents expect. For example, while John wants to play football and go out on dates, the parents do not allow either activity because they fear that he may become distracted from his studies. In addition, dating is seen as an inappropriate activity for an adolescent. The counselor then decides to contact the parents.

While speaking with the parents, the counselor learns that they are very embarrassed about John's failing grades and signs of depression. The counselor also learns that the parents are rarely at home. The father is a construction worker during the day and drives a taxi in the evening, whereas the mother is a cook at a Korean restaurant. They believe that academic achievement is the most important goal for their son. The counselor decides to intervene.

At first, the counselor successfully puts the parents at ease by gently acknowledging the parents' embarrassment over their son's difficulties and reminding them that their son has generally been a good student in the past. The counselor convinces the parents that there is a very good possibility that the problem can be resolved with the assistance of everyone involved, including the friend and the teacher. With support from John's parents and permission from John, the counselor decides to conduct a counseling session with everyone involved.

During the meeting, the parents are encouraged to discuss their thoughts and feelings about what has been happening. With some reluctance, the parents are able to express their concerns about their disharmonious relationship with John and his lack of academic achievement. In return, John, with encouragement from his friend and the counselor, expresses that he feels lonely at home and that he wants to expand his social network. He also informs his parents that he wants to be more like his American friends in the types of activities that he is involved in. After many sessions involving further discussion and negotiations, John and his parents agree that John will have greater freedom if he can maintain satisfactory grades. The parents, teacher, and the counselor also agree that they will monitor John more closely and will provide assistance when needed.

## References

Harvey, Y. S. K., & Chung, S. H. (1980). The Koreans. In J. F. McDermott, Jr., W.S. Tseng, & T. W. Maretzki, (Eds.), *People and cultures of Hawaii: A psychocultural profile* (pp. 135-154). Honolulu, HI: The University Press of Hawaii.

Korean Overseas Information Service. (1990). *A handbook of Korea.* Seoul: Author.

Lee, J. C., & Cynn, V. E. H. (1991). Issues in counseling 1.5 generation Korean Americans. In C. C. Lee & B. L. Richardson (Eds.), *Multicultural issues in counseling: New approaches to diversity* (pp. 127-140). Alexandria, VA: American Association for Counseling and Development.

Lee, D. C. & Lee, E. H. (1990). Korean immigrant families in American: Role and value conflict. In H. C. Kim & E. H. Lee (Eds.), *Koreans in American: Dreams and realities* (pp. 72-82). Seoul: Institute of Korean Studies.

Locke, D. C. (1992). Increasing multicultural understanding: A comprehensive model. In P. Pedersen (Series Ed.), *Multicultural aspects of counseling series 1* (pp. 113-126). Newbury Park, CA: Sage.

U.S. Bureau of the Census. (1990). *1990 Census of Population, General Population Characteristics, United States.* Washington, D.C.: U.S. Government Printing Office.

# Counseling College Students from Taiwan

*Jun-chih Gisela Lin*

## Overview

According to the Institute of International Education, 37,581 college students from Taiwan were in the United States in 1993-1994, making them the third largest group among the international student population (Davis, 1994). Of these, 65.5% were graduate students, 29.4% were undergraduates, and 5% were classified as Other.

## Common Stressors

In studying the initial adjustment of students from Taiwan, Ying and Liese (1991) reported that over half of the 171 participants experienced a decline in emotional well-being. Academic adjustment is the major priority for Taiwanese students. Coming to a new country, they often experience difficulties with academic advisors, instructors' teaching styles, language barriers, financial pressure, discrimination, loneliness, relationship issues, nonassertiveness, performance anxiety, depression, paranoia, bi-cultural conflicts, safety concerns, worries about political movements and family situations in Taiwan, employment concerns upon graduation, and anxiety about reentry adjustment (if they are planning to return).

## Within Group Differences

Taiwanese differ among themselves in numerous ways:

1. racial/ethnic backgrounds (e.g., Taiwanese, Chinese from China around 1949, Taiwan Chinese, Hakka, the nine tribes of Taiwan's aboriginal peoples);
2. dialects (Mandarin, Taiwanese, Hakka, native Taiwan's aboriginal dialects);
3. religions (Buddhists, Taoists, Protestants, Catholics, Moslems, Mormons, Atheists);
4. political beliefs (e.g., the Nationalist Party of China, the Democratic Progressive Party, the Chinese New Party, the Independent Party, the Green Party);
5. social economic status (e.g., family income, parents' occupations and education levels);
6. geographical locations (e.g., urban, rural, south, north, west, east); and
7. sexual orientation (rarely verbalized if not heterosexual).

Furthermore, the way in which Taiwanese students are referred to can be a highly sensitive issue. A survey by the Democratic Progressive Party reported on May 13, 1995 in the *World Journal*, a Chinese newspaper, indicated that 35.3% of adults in Taiwan don't consider themselves Taiwanese, 29% don't consider themselves Chinese, 27.2% think they are both, and 6.5% "don't know who they are." Therefore, when working with students from Taiwan, it is important to verify their identities rather than refer to them all as "Taiwanese." In spite of these differences, the people of Taiwan are similar in that they are influenced by Confucius' teachings, Buddhism, and Taoism.

## Implementation of Programs

Effective programs involve the collaborative efforts of international student advisors, academic advisors, major professors, English language instructors, student leaders, community leaders, and counselors to assist the international students throughout the stages of pre-arrival, initial adjustment, and on-going adjustment. Some of the specific ways in which programs can help Taiwanese students are by orienting them to:

1. the university system,
2. instructors' different teaching styles, and
3. the adjustment process.

Examples of helping the adjustment process include offering mentors or role models, providing opportunities for social or support groups with other international and domestic students to enhance multicultural understanding, and promoting integration into the academic community. Cross-cultural programs help students with bicultural conflicts to achieve a balance between participating in the new culture and maintaining their own cultural identities, and with readjustment back to their home country (Paige, 1990).

### Counseling Implications and Strategies

Taiwanese students in general are likely to seek help for "academic concerns" even though their problems may not be primarily academic (e.g., loss of interests, lack of motivation, or laziness may be symptoms of depression; Lin, 1993). They are more comfortable with counselors who function like an "educator" because students in Taiwan usually are counseled by their classroom teachers. Culturally sensitive counseling should be easily accessible. Twenty-four hour telephone hotlines (e.g., Lifeline, Teacher Zhang) are more widely used by Taiwan people than face-to-face counseling for crisis intervention, consultation, and referrals because the telephone hotline is more accessible and "face saving."

Modifying traditional counseling approaches so that they are more flexible is crucial when working with Chinese/Taiwanese. Lin (1989, 1993) suggests that counseling strategies be modified to be more consistent with the students' needs and expectations at the first contact. Her suggestions include:

1. collect only the necessary relevant information and resolve the students' most immediate problems;
2. acknowledge cultural differences;
3. be warm, empathic, nonjudgemental, personal; and
4. be willing to self-disclose to establish trust.

If the student has specific concerns, use a direct, concrete, practical, well-structured approach, and allow for longer silences. If the problem is related to adjustment, explain the adjustment process and deal with anxiety and depression symptoms associated with adjustment stress by helping them understand the mind-body relationship. Normalizing their problems and redefining problem areas as being bilingual and bicultural helps them to regain self-confidence. Sharing similar experiences of others emphasizes the "normality" of their concerns. After establishing a relationship, be more subtle and indirect when confrontation is necessary (e.g., "Other people in similar situations often experience..., do you yourself have similar experiences?"). With regard to social support, find out what support system they have and what else they need. Within their cultural beliefs, support systems may include concepts such as "destiny" and receiving advice from "fortune tellers." It is not unreasonable to assume that if a Taiwanese student comes for counseling, the student is in crisis even though it may not appear so. Develop culturally appropriate self-help materials like brochures, audio tapes, video tapes, computer programs, and educational slides, using Chinese language whenever possible. Offer consultation and referrals through the telephone, electronic media, newsletters, and newspaper columns.

### Case Study

Ming was a first-semester, single, female graduate student from Taiwan in her mid-20's, referred by a program that works with international students. The first contact was an e-mail she sent to a Taiwan Chinese counselor asking for available resources that would help her to improve her English. She did not pass the oral skills part of the English Language Placement Examination (ELPE).

In an e-mail reply to Ming, the counselor offered a walk-in counseling service (no time restrictions, and no appointment needed), and the International Students Group. The International Students Group is semi-structured, psycho-educational, and based on the assumptions that international students are goal oriented and respond positively to structure. It addresses common academic, cultural, psychological, and social issues international students often encounter.

Ming's first in-person contact was through the walk-in counseling service. The session was conducted in Mandarin Chinese, complying with the client's preference. The counselor shared her own experiences about how she improved her English speaking skills by speaking in classes even though it was difficult in terms of culture and being female. The counselor emphasized that the International Students Group provided similar English speaking opportunities. Since Ming had to take another oral exam soon, she agreed to come to the group. In the group, she realized many others had similar adjustment problems. With encouragement, she responded to questions such as, "How is this issue played out in Taiwan?"

Ming came to the group three times, and met with the counselor individually two more times for process and follow-up. She became more self-confident, more social, began to network with the Chinese community, and passed her ELPE exam.

With the aid of self-disclosure and Ming's language of choice, the counselor validated Ming's experiences and addressed her immediate concerns. This encouraged Ming to use other services. The group helped Ming to understand that her problems were "normal" for bilingual/bicultural people in transition.

### References

Davis, T. M. (Ed.). (1994). *Open doors 1993/1994: Report on international educational exchange.* New York: Institute of International Education.

Lin, J. C. G. (1989). *Counseling Chinese/Chinese Americans.* Unpublished manuscript, University of Massachusetts, Amherst.

Lin, J. C. G. (1993). *College Survival Skills Group Manual for Culturally Different Students.* Unpublished internship specialty project, University of Houston, Houston.

Paige, M. (1990). International Students: Cross-Cultural Psychological Perspectives. In R. W. Brislin (Ed.), *Applied Cross-Cultural Psychology* (pp. 161-185). Newbury Park, California: Sage Publications.

Ying, Y. W., & Liese, L. (1991). Emotional well-being of Taiwan students in the U.S.: An examination of pre- to post-arrival differential. *International Journal of Intercultural Relations, 15* (3), 345-366.

# White Racism

*Michael J. D'Andrea*

### Overview

Many White Americans think of racism as something that occurred in the 1960s. However, the increasing incidence of racial violence and harassment reportedly occurring in our cities and on many university campuses provide disturbing evidence that racial hatred and discrimination have never been adequately addressed.

The disproportionate number of African American, Latino, and Native American persons who are unemployed, undereducated, in prisons, and living in poverty in the 1990s represent additional examples of the ways in which racism continues to be perpetuated in this country. Other indicators of this ongoing national dilemma include both the apathetic and increasingly hostile reactions many White Americans have to the types of problems that have been listed above (D'Andrea & Daniels, 1994). Racism is a learned response which can be extended or reduced depending on the quality of one's environmental interactions and experiences. Counselors can play a crucial role in ameliorating racism in society by influencing the environments in which they work. To do so, however, counselors must first have a comprehensive understanding of the different ways racism is commonly manifested.

### Defining Racism

The word "racism" has been defined in many ways in the professional literature. Some of the central elements in these definitions include the following points:

1. Racism involves prejudicial and stereotypic thinking about persons from different racial backgrounds.
2. Racism is rooted in the belief that race is a primary determinant of human traits and capacities.
3. Racism is built on the notion that racial differences produce an inherent superiority of a particular race.
4. Racism refers to the use of power to carry out discriminatory practices in a variety of social settings and institutions.

Some of the more conspicuous ways in which institutional racism continues to exist in the United States are noted in housing patterns; segregated schools and churches; discriminatory employment and promotion policies; the continued control of the mass media by White persons, and the use of textbooks and other curriculum materials in schools which provide an inaccurate portrayal of the history and lifestyles of persons from non-white backgrounds (Kozol, 1991).

### A Comprehensive Model of Racism

While the most blatant forms of racism typically receive the greatest media attention, this destructive psychosocial dynamic also occurs in a variety of more subtle but equally harmful ways. Locke (1992) provides a comprehensive model of racism that may be useful when considering ways of dealing with the manifestation of racism. This model is comprised of four qualitatively different types of racism that are briefly described below.

### Overt/Intentional Racism

*Overt/intentional racism* is manifested in purposeful and open demonstration of hatred for individuals from non-white backgrounds. Images of Ku Klux Klan members and angry "skinhead" youths assaulting persons of color without any apparent provocation typify this sort of racism.

Counselors are encouraged to take a proactive role in helping prevent this form of racism from occurring in schools and communities. This can be achieved, in part, by working with others (i.e., students, principals, parents, community leaders, etc.) to develop explicit policies that prohibit physical, verbal, and/or psychological assaults against others because of their cultural/ethnic/racial background, and which include a clearly stated set of consequences for violating such policies.

### Overt/Unintentional Racism

*Overt/unintentional racism* refers to public behaviors that, while genuinely not intended to be disrespectful, are clearly interpreted by others as being racially insensitive and discriminatory. An incident that occurred during Ross Perot's 1992 presidential campaign provides an example of how this sort of racism can occur.

In a major address given at the annual convention of the National Association for the Advancement of Colored People (NAACP) in Nashville, Tennessee, Mr. Perot repeatedly used the phrase "you people" when making several points about the predominately African American audience to whom he was speaking. Although apparently very sincere about his intent to present his views in a respectful manner, Mr. Perot was visibly shaken by the negative reactions he received from the African Americans attending this meeting. When interviewed by reporters immediately following his speech, a number of persons pointed out that Perot's statements were racially discriminatory and demeaning.

Overt/unintentional racism reflects an individual's lack of awareness as to why seemingly "ordinary" statements generate a sense of insult and anger in many non-white persons.

Counselors can do a number of things to reduce peoples' tendency to exhibit overt/unintentional racism. This includes initiating multicultural education projects in schools, conducting anti-racist training seminars, and working in small groups with persons from different racial backgrounds who are willing to discuss instances in which they experienced overt/unintentional racism in their own lives.

### Covert/Intentional Racism

White persons tend to underestimate the degree to which *covert/intentional racism* occurs in modern society. Because it is manifested in covert ways, it is more subtle than overt/intentional or overt/unintentional racism.

Using tests that are culturally biased in order to select individuals for educational programs or employment positions is a common example of covert/intentional racism in action. This sort of racism continues to be institutionalized and widely practiced in many universities and businesses across the United States. Counselors can have a positive impact in addressing covert/intentional racism by supporting equal employment opportunity policies and by helping to eliminate culturally/biased test scores as criteria in making academic and/or employment decisions.

### Covert/Unintentional Racism

*Covert/unintentional racism* refers to those behaviors which, though unintended, often allow racial discrimination and insensitivity to go unchallenged. The lack of interest and support for the multicultural counseling movement among many White counselors represents one type of covert/unintentional racism that exits in the counseling profession. Three factors underscore the existence of this sort of racism in the profession. First, professional counselors know that rapid cultural/ethnic/racial diversification of the United States characterizes our modern society. As a result of this social reality, an increasing number of counselors are called upon to provide services to persons from diverse cultural, ethnic, and racial backgrounds with whom they have little knowledge or experience.

Second, numerous research publications have clearly indicated that many traditional counseling approaches are not effective (and in some cases are even harmful) when used among culturally and racially diverse client populations (Atkinson, Morten, & Sue, 1993; Pedersen, 1988). These findings support the notion that counselors need to embrace the multicultural counseling movement in order to learn more effective ways of serving persons from diverse backgrounds.

Third, despite the apparent need to embrace the multicultural counseling movement, many White counselors are reluctant to recognize multiculturalism as "the fourth force" in the profession (Pedersen, 1988). Frequently, this reluctance is accompanied by an internalized resistance to commit oneself to develop new counseling competencies which are necessary to work effectively and respectfully with persons from non-White backgrounds.

This reluctance and resistance reflects the types of attitudes that underlie much of the covert/unintentional racism which exists in the counseling profession. Counselors who exhibit covert/unintentional racism in these ways typically exhibit a culturally encapsulated view of counseling which perpetuates the inappropriate use of many counseling theories and interventions among persons of color (Wrenn, 1985).

White counselors can help reduce the level of covert/unintentional racism in the profession in two inter-related ways. First, they can actively strive to demonstrate a genuine commitment to increase their own multicultural counseling awareness, knowledge, and skills by seeking out professional development training opportunities in this area. Second, White counselors can exhibit enthusiastic support for multiculturalism as the recognized "fourth force" in the profession (Pedersen, 1988). This can, in part, be done by becoming an active member in the Association for Multicultural Counseling and Development, an official division of the American Counseling Association.

The following brief case study provides examples of the ways in which racism may be manifested by counselors. The specific types of racism evinced by the counselor in this case study have been identified in parentheses.

## Case Study

Beth, a European-American and John, an African American, are sophomores in high school and are good friends. They are involved in several school activities together and often go out on weekends with other friends. John asks Beth to go with him to a school dance and Beth readily agrees. She was excited when she told one of her counselors about her plans, but the counselor seemed somewhat upset (overt unintentional). The counselor explained that Beth might be a

disappointment to her parents (covert intentional) and would certainly be the subject of school gossip if she were to date an African American (covert intentional). When Beth inquired as to what she should do, the counselor encouraged her to cancel the date (overt intentional).

## Conclusion

In closing, much more discussion and research is urgently needed to further our understanding of the problem of racism. However, increased awareness and knowledge of racism must be supported by the moral, political, and professional resolve to engage in activities that are aimed at effectively addressing this insidious psychosocial problem in our nation.

## References

Atkinson, D. R., Morten, G., & Sue, D. W. (1993). *Counseling American minorities* (4th ed.). Dubuque, IA: Brown & Benchmark.

D'Andrea, M., & Daniels, J. (1994). The different faces of racism in higher education. *Thought and Action, 10* (1), 73-90.

Kozol, J. (1991). *Savage inequalities: Children in America's schools.* New York: Crown Publishers, Inc.

Locke, D. C. (1992). *Increasing multicultural understanding.* Thousand Oaks, CA: Sage.

Pedersen, P. (1988). *A handbook for developing multicultural awareness.* Alexandria, VA: American Association for Counseling and Development.

Wrenn, C. G. (1985). Afterward: The culturally encapsulated counselor revisited. In P. Pedersen (Ed.), *Handbook of cross cultural counseling and therapy* (pp. 323-329). Westport, CT: Greenwood Press.

# Demographic, Status and Affiliation Cultures

# Counseling Athletes

*Albert J. Petitpas*
*Britton W. Brewer*
*Judy L. Van Raalte*

### Overview

Although athletic participation cuts across gender, ethnic, and racial boundaries, athletes comprise a readily definable social group with a unique set of norms, beliefs, and patterns of interaction. From youth sport to masters level competition, millions of people around the world engage in some type of sport activity. Although proponents of sport participation have argued that involvement in sport builds character and enhances personal development, this notion is being met with increasing skepticism. Concerns about the academic, personal, and social development of athletes have created a demand for counseling professionals who are sensitive to the concerns of this special population (Danish, Petitpas, & Hale, 1993).

### Society's Treatment of Athletes

Athletes are in the unique position of being both revered and derogated. As public figures, many athletes are treated as superstars but they can also be stereotyped as "dumb jocks" who are overprotected and pampered by the athletic system (Engstrom & Sedlacek, 1991). Athletes, particularly black athletes, can be exploited and victimized by a sports system that demands undivided loyalties, enormous amounts of time and energy, and numerous personal and social sacrifices, with little hope for a career in professional sports (Edwards, 1983). Thus, athletes are viewed simultaneously as superheroes, victims, spoiled children, and role models.

### Special Problems

Although athletes share the same types of concerns faced by the general population, there are several within- and between-group differences.

Research has indicated that athletes may differ by gender, race, and type of sport (e.g., revenue producing versus non-revenue producing) on several factors, including career maturity, academic preparation, substance abuse, steroid use, susceptibility to eating disorders, and sex-role stereotyping (Etzel, Ferrante, & Pinkney, 1991). Athletes compete in a highly visible, stressful, time-consuming environment where their daily performances are often a matter of public record. As a result, they face the normal developmental concerns of the general population, but with additional stressors and less spare time. This combination of factors may account for the fact that college-aged athletes have been found to lag behind their age mates on developmental factors, such as educational planning, career planning, and engaging in mature relationships with peers (Sowa & Gressard, 1983).

In addition, the various demands of athletic participation may leave college-aged athletes in a position where engaging in exploratory behavior is not seen as feasible or necessary. A strong, exclusive commitment to the athletic role has been shown to be positively related to psychological distress when athletes experience threats to their sport participation (Brewer, 1993). Unfortunately, injury and the team selection process are an ever-present fact of life for most competitive athletes. Although the longevity of an athletic career varies by sport, most athletes are forced to retire at a time when their age-mates are still developing their careers. Most athletes who aspire to elite amateur or professional sports careers find it necessary to devote virtually all of their time and energy toward preparing for their athletic goals. Counselors who are aware of the unique demands of athletic participation may be particularly important for athletes who are experiencing role conflict (e.g., balancing student and athlete roles) and for athletes who are disengaging from sport. The counselor's sensitivity and rapport can be enhanced by the following:

1. attending practices and competitions;
2. learning the language and rules of the sport;
3. becoming knowledgeable about the sport
   culture (e.g., social interactions, player/coach relationships); and
4. acknowledging athletes' strong self-investment in sport.

### Availability of Support Services

In general, counseling support services for athletes have been either underutilized, as is the case for college student-athletes, or unavailable, as is the case for most athletes of other age groups. As already suggested, college athletes may have little time, energy, or need to seek out counseling assistance. They have an identity on campus and a busy, regulated life-style. In addition, athletes often learn through sport participation that it is a sign of weakness to seek out help and that strong athletes "just tough it out." Athletes may be prone to deny problems (the macho factor) or they may attempt to medicate them away through the use and/or abuse of alcohol (Etzel et al., 1991).

Recently, there has been a trend within the academic-athletic support services at major universities to recruit new staff members with specific skills in career and personal counseling. These counselors, working within the athletic department's academic support system, are introduced as a part of the normal academic-athletic support services with the hope of bypassing any stigma that may be attached to going to the university counseling center for assistance. The National Collegiate Athletic Association (NCAA) has also developed a "Life Skills Program," which has a goal of helping college athletes acquire specific skills to better equip them to deal with the stressors of being a student-athlete. These programs are relatively new efforts and evidence of their effectiveness is not yet available.

For the most part, formal counseling services

for non-college athletes are random, isolated efforts. There are promising developments on several fronts that warrant some optimism, however. Several national youth sport organizations (e.g., Pop Warner Football and Cheerleading) have added a sport psychology component to their coach education programs that teach coaches strategies to help young athletes get more psychosocial benefit from their athletic participation. The NCAA Youth Education Through Sport (YES) program has added a life skills enrichment component for young athletes who participate in YES sport clinics. Similar efforts are underway with several Olympic teams (e.g., U.S. Swimming and Diving), and a number of professional sports organizations have instituted player assistance programs. Although these efforts are encouraging, more systematic programs are necessary, particularly those with a primary prevention and enhancement orientation.

### Implications for Practice, Training, and Research

As support services for athletes have expanded from an athletic performance enhancement orientation to a more educational/developmental perspective, the overlap with counseling training and philosophy becomes more apparent. In fact, the Association for the Advancement of Applied Sport Psychology (AAASP), which is the only organization to certify applied sport psychologists, has a strong counseling component as one of the major competencies for certification. It is clear that counseling competencies are essential in working with athletes, but they may not be sufficient.

Danish et al. (1993) recommended that beyond the basic counseling and listening skills, professionals who work with athletes should acquire training and supervised experience that affords opportunities to:

1. learn about the role of psychosocial factors in sports;
2. teach life skills to athletes and teams;
3. counsel individual athletes and groups of athletes using an enhancement approach; and
4. design, implement, and evaluate an

enhancement program with a group of athletes.

Furthermore, a knowledge base in the sport sciences (e.g., sport psychology, exercise physiology, motor learning) and experience as a coach, player, or exercise participant would further enhance a counselor's understanding of the athletic experience.

### Case Study

In 1988, the United States Olympic Committee created the Career Assistance Program for Athletes (CAPA) to assist Olympic-level athletes in preparing for their retirement from active sport competition. Participants ranged in age from 14 to 47 and represented a wide range of sports, cultural groups, and socioeconomic levels. In general, participants were likely to believe that they had no marketable skills. They often felt alone and misunderstood, and were hard pressed to identify support resources that could assist them in the retirement process. Many athletes were frustrated and angry at the politics of the Olympic system, but were fearful to invest energy in career exploration because it might detract from their sport performance. To deal with these concerns, a series of workshops were offered which were co-facilitated by athletic counseling professionals and elite athletes who had gone through a training program. Small group interactions focused on managing the emotional and social impact of disengagement from competitive sport, and introduced the components of life-work planning.

Evaluations of the CAPA program revealed that participants increased their knowledge of the career development process and they identified many transferable skills. Participants rated the social support received from other CAPA athletes and their increased career knowledge as instrumental in developing a greater sense of career self-efficacy.

### Conclusion

Athletes are a diverse group with unique concerns. Counselors with an understanding of the athletic experience and possessing solid counseling skills are in an excellent position to assist athletes in reaching their academic, athletic, career, and social potential.

### References

Brewer, B. W. (1993). Self-identity and specific vulnerability to depressed mood. *Journal of Personality, 61,* 343-364.

Danish, S. J., Petitpas, A. J., & Hale B. D. (1993). Life development intervention for athletes: Life skills through sports. *The Counseling Psychologist, 21,* 352-385.

Edwards, H. (1983). The exploitation of black athletes. *AGB Reports, 28,* 37-48.

Engstrom, C. M., & Sedlacek, W. E. (1991). A study of prejudice toward university student-athletes. *Journal of Counseling and Development, 70,* 189-193.

Etzel, E. F., Ferrante, A. P., & Pinkney, J. W. (Eds.). (1991). *Counseling college student athletes: Issues and interventions.* Morgantown, WV: Fitness Information Technology.

Sowa, C. J., & Gressard, C. F. (1983). Athletic participation: Its relationship to student development. *Journal of College Student Personnel, 24,* 236-239.

# Counseling People with Traumatic Brain Injury

*Masahiro Nochi*
*Mary Handley*

### Overview

In summer 1993, more than one thousand people from throughout the country gathered in Washington D.C. for a demonstration. They were individuals with traumatic brain injuries (TBI) and their families. These demonstrators were pushing congress to pass a bill that would secure federal support for TBI rehabilitation and community living. The demonstration suggested that many people with TBI identify themselves as a group, a subculture with unique needs. This chapter discusses critical issues regarding counseling this population as a cultural group.

### Demographics

TBI results from an external physical impact to the brain, which is often produced in traffic accidents, falls, or violent crimes. Anually, between 80,000 - 85,000 persons suffer a TBI in this country, with twice as many males being affected as females. The majority of TBI occur between the ages of 16 and 25 (Kraus & Sorenson, 1994). Due to the age of this population, counselors need to address vocational, educational, and social issues.

### Unique Problems and Stressors

Symptoms accompanied by brain injuries are varied depending upon the location and size of the injury (Heilman & Valenstein, 1993). People with TBI generally have diffuse damage in two or more locations of the brain. Consequently, they are likely to sustain complex combinations of the symptoms, with no two individuals ever experiencing the same symptoms. Several groups of functional difficulties exist, which include: physical changes, such as paralysis of the limbs; sensory/perceptual changes, such as visual field defects; cognitive changes, such as memory and attention disorders; and emotional/personality changes, such as aggression and depression.

### Common Experiences and the Group Identity

Despite individual differences, individuals who survive TBI have many common experiences (Crisp, 1992; Kaplan, 1993). They undergo the dramatic disruption of their lives, and they attend therapy during the recovery stages. Also, they are likely to have difficulty in readjusting to their home or school environments and work places due to the cognitive, emotional, and personality changes. A feeling of isolation from society or community is common since social and/or intimate relationships are difficult to maintain or rebuild. They may call themselves "survivors" distinguishing themselves entirely from "the disabled" population. Similar to the deaf population, it seems that TBI survivors are beginning to create their own sub-culture and their own communities.

### Currently Developing Programs

Recently, several programs have been developed to meet the needs of people with TBI, not only in the acute, medical settings but also in the community (Kreutzer & Wehman, 1990). After medical rehabilitation, for instance, the individual may be able to use "transitional living programs" in which he or she can learn living and job skills. Some communities provide "independent living services," which range from attendant care and adapted housing/transportation to advocacy and removal of environmental barriers. In the field of vocational rehabilitation, "supported employment programs" are beginning to produce good results for this population. People with severe TBI can join the competitive job market when they receive the careful support of a job coach and/or co-workers (Ellerd, Moor, Speer, & Lackey, 1994).

Counseling from professionals or peers plays a crucial role in these programs.

### Accessibility to Services

However, accessibility to service programs is often limited, depending on insurance coverage and geographic location. Payment for counseling services during inpatient rehabilitation is generally not an issue. But when the individual returns home, to his or her community, frequently there are no such programs, or there are no funds for payment. The individual may not be able to find information about programs, funding sources, or appropriately trained professionals. Most states have a state-wide Brain Injury Association, and often local support groups for people with TBI and their families exist in many regions. The support groups can provide information about community resources as well as peer counseling.

### Implications for Counseling Practice

In order to meet the special needs of this subculture, the following points should be considered (Cicerone, 1989; Lewington, 1993; Pollack, 1994):

1. Carefully prepare a counseling environment which is free from noise and has adequate lighting, seating, and ventilation. The client may be easily irritated or distracted by environmental conditions.
2. Spend enough time to establish good rapport with the client. It takes a while for a counselor to understand a client's behavioral characteristics and special needs, and for the client to feel secure in the counseling setting.
3. Translate and explain the medical and neuropsychological information to the client or his or her family. They may be relieved when they learn that they are not to blame for their problems but that their brain pathology is.
4. Help the client to become aware of his or her residual capacities or strengths. This awareness increases problem-solving skills and enhances the client's self-esteem.
5. Use both directive and indirective

counseling techniques, depending on the client's characteristics. When a client's cognitive abilities are limited, start with the directive/educational approach.

6. Attend not only to the neurological symptoms, but also to the client's interpretation of the symptoms. The discrepancy between "objective" description and the client's interpretation is often related to the client's concerns or those of his or her family.
7. Find appropriate communication channels through which the client can express his or her thoughts and emotions. Besides verbal or written communication, artistic means such as poems, songs, pictures, and videotaping may be helpful.
8. Use more feedbacks in order to secure the communication and to facilitate the client's self-exploration. The counselor's frequent repetition and summarizing can help the client to concentrate on one topic.
9. Do not overdiagnose the pathology. It is always possible that the client's behavior is influenced by environmental conditions, including what the counselor says or does.
10. Consider the change of environmental conditions to solve the client's problems. The client may be able to use social, community, and family resources to eliminate problems and to achieve his or her goals.
11. Locate peer counseling for the client. He or she may be interested in information about a TBI sub-culture and may want support from people in similar situations.
12. Include the whole family in the counseling process. Generally, this type of injury affects the entire family. They influence the individual's rehabilitation outcomes in many ways.

### Case Study

A 30-year-old woman, Helen, sustains a severe TBI as a result of a motor vehicle accident. At the time of the accident, she worked at a hospital as an LPN and lived with her significant other and her two children from a previous marriage. Her brain injury affects her ability to walk, her speech, and her control of emotions. She often becomes overstimulated, confused, and has trouble focusing her attention on one task.

She is in a rehabilitation program and requires 24-hour care. Her physician expects her to improve and to eventually return to her home, provided that she has the proper support. Her parents and siblings are distressed and concerned about the changes in her personality and her future. Her significant other is attempting to remove himself from the entire situation which will result in financial and emotional hardship for Helen. Helen does not understand what is going on and wants only to go home.

The counseling issues are the following: educate Helen and her family about her medical status, brain injury, and rehabilitation program; work with both Helen and her significant other to help her understand what he is feeling; facilitate positive visits and counseling sessions with her two sons; assist her with issues regarding her employment and eventual return to work; help her identify her priorities for the next several months; and begin to investigate potential support in the community.

Due to the complexity of TBI rehabilitation, a counselor requires specific skills and knowledge. For more information, contact the Brain Injury Association, 1776 Massachusetts Avenue, Washington DC, 20036, or (202) 296-6483, (800) 400-6443.

### References

Cicerone, K. D. (1989). Psychotherapeutic interventions with traumatically brain-injured patients. *Rehabilitation Psychology, 34,* 105-114.

Crisp, R. (1992). Return to work after traumatic brain injury. *Journal of Rehabilitation, 58* (4), 27-33.

Ellerd, D., Moor, S., Speer, D., & Lackey, R. D. (1994). Nontraditional support in supported employment: Preliminary results for individuals with TBI. *Journal of Applied Rehabilitation Counseling, 25* (4), 22-25.

Heilman, K. M., & Valenstein, E. (Eds.). (1993). *Clinical neuropsychology* (3rd ed.). New York: Oxford University Press.

Kaplan, S. P. (1993). Five-year tracking of psychosocial changes in people with severe traumatic brain injury. *Rehabilitation Counseling Bulletin, 36,* 151-159.

Kraus, J. F., & Sorenson, S. B. (1994). Epidemiology. In J. M. Silver, S. C. Yudofsky, & R. E. Hales (Eds.), *Neuropsychiatry of traumatic brain injury* (pp. 3-41). Washington DC: American Psychiatric Press.

Kreutzer, J. S., & Wehman, C. F. (Eds.). (1990). *Community integration following traumatic brain injury.* Baltmore, MD: Paul H. Brooks.

Lewington, P. J. (1993). Counseling survivors of traumatic brain injury. *Canadian Journal of Counseling, 27* (4), 274-288.

Pollack, I. W. (1994). Individual psychotherapy. In J. M. Silver, S. C. Yudofsky, & R. E. Hales (Eds.), *Neuropsychiatry of traumatic brain injury* (pp. 671-702). Washington DC: American Psychiatric Press.

# Counseling Buddhist Clients

*Wanpen Murgatroyd*

### Overview

Counselors need to understand Buddhism's belief systems and guidelines for social conduct since they are the foundation of the Buddhist Asian American's group identity and world view. Buddhists' differing world views and social rules underlie a multitude of their problems in the Western world. Examples and recommendations are described to assist counselors working with this group of clients.

### Salient Buddhist Concepts

Buddhism is both a system of beliefs and a practical teaching of social conduct. The topic is vast and complicated, thus, only three salient concepts are presented here, selected for their major contributions to the group identity of Buddhist Asian Americans.

First is a belief in the law of "kamma" which is a natural law of cause and effect or action and result. All actions inevitably lead to results proportionate in nature and degree to the deed. Kamma can be committed through body, speech, and thought. The consequences of an action may be immediate and explicit, however, often they are not.

Second is the law of "conditionality" that governs the interrelatedness and interdependence of all things: how things change and decay; how life is characterized by existential conditions of birth, old age, disease, and death; how things are impermanent, arise, exist, and cease depending on causes and conditions. Thus, a permanent self is not possible. Last is the law of "samsara," which is the cycle of birth and death. The present life is not the only one, and it does not dissolve into nothingness at death. The process and the continuity of life are sustained by the force of

kamma (Ajahn Chah, 1982; Buddhadasa Bhikkhu, 1988; Plamintr, 1994).

### Group Identity and World View

In general, Buddhist Asian American group identity is influenced by the Buddhist concepts of kamma, samsara, and the interdependency and connectedness of all things. These concepts, in turn, form the foundation of their relationships within their immediate families, extended families, and communities at large.

Buddhism affirms and reinforces relationships of interdependency by teaching compassion, tolerance, acceptance, contemplation, self-restraint, and detachment. These teachings instill the basic values of cooperation and harmonious relationships. A good person is defined by the quality of her or his relationships with other fellow beings in general, and family members in particular (Nguyen, 1984; Plamintr, 1994; Ratanasuwan, 1972). Buddhist Asian Americans look at the world and interact with others through these views.

### Unique Problems

The multitude of problems faced by Buddhist Asian Americansis an inherent consequence of a world view that differs from that of the Western world.The problems can be clustered in the following manner (Jayatilleke, 1987; Nguyen, 1984; Owen, 1985):

1. *Relationships:* The belief in inter-dependency and connectedness encourages asking for help and depending on others at times of crisis and difficulty. The family is turned to first, then friends, neighbors, members of a common temple, teachers, employers, social services, and society at large. Buddhists

are also willing to give back what they received. A relationship is formed on the basis of an ability to give and take. On the contrary, the Western world view is more limited. One is responsible for one's own problems. Every person is an island: separate, self-contained, autonomous, free, and independent. Westerners view relationships with Buddhist Asian Americans as needy and excessively demanding. This leaves the Buddhist Asian American with a feeling of isolation and alienation.

2. *Communication/Interaction:* The communication style of the Buddhist Asian American is intrinsically shaped by self- and emotional-restraint, indirectness, acceptance, and reflectiveness. The intention of what is said is more important than the accuracy of execution. The American style of "speaking one's mind" is, thus, often misunderstood and even hurtful. On the contrary, the Buddhist Asian American is perceived as shy, weak, unassertive, unintelligent, indecisive, and incomprehensible.

3. *Problem Solving Process:* Buddhism teaches acceptance and tolerance towards self, others, and life. Problems and difficulties are recognized, accepted, and lived with. It is not necessary to try continually to change or control life events. Change is a natural law. It is only necessary to recognize and accept the universal change which governs life, and thus, live in harmony with the cosmic way. This kind of problem solving is misunderstood by the Western culture as passive, pessimistic, and is perceived as a type of learned helplessness.

Because of these varying concepts in relationships, communication, and perception of problems, a therapeutic relationship may not develop. The following example illustrates this point.

### Case Study

Lee is at the end of his senior year in computer science. He requests to see a career counselor in order to prepare for a job search after graduation. The counselor gives him several tests and helps him understand the process of searching for a job. In the third session, Lee gives the counselor his resume and asks her to edit it for him. The counselor explains that it is not her job and that Lee should pay someone else to do this. Lee does not come back to counseling. The counselor finally calls and requests that he come in for a termination session. Lee is hurt and feels that the counselor does not care for him, but he comes in at her request and indicates that he is pleased with her advice. He has found someone to help him with the resume.

Lee's counselor, from her Western world view, sees his request as an inappropriate behavior that needs to be changed. Lee, on the other hand, interprets her action as uncaring and no longer trusts her. However, his culture, valuing tolerance, does not encourage confrontation. He, therefore, feels obligated to respond to her request and indirectly communicates his anger.

### Recommendations for Counselors

1. Express genuine concern for the client's discrepancies and conflicts by asking for explanations and listening carefully without judging, intervening, or interrupting.
2. Accept the client's explanation from his or her cultural reference point without an assumption of right or wrong.
3. Understand the client's expectations of the counselor and counseling from his or hercultural reference point.
4. Understand the different meanings and definitions of relationships and differing communication styles.
5. Establish common ground as a basis for a working relationship.
6. Do not assume that all Buddhist Asian Americans will react the same way.

### Successful Programs

There are no mental health programs tailored for the unique problems of Buddhist Asian Americans. However, there are mental health services embedded in more broadly used programs such as social services and general health care. One worthy of note is Mutual Assistance Associations (MAAs) which emerged from the Southeast Asian refugee community in the United States. MAAs are community-based programs patterned on the model of the extended family (Owen, 1985).

## Action Plans

In developing effective mental health services for this group, their social structure must be kept in mind. The few researchers (Canda & Phaobtong, 1992; Nguyen, 1984; Owen, 1985) who have investigated the components necessary to provide effective services to this group seem to agree on the following:

1. The use of pre-existing natural support networks such as the extended family, and community resources such as MAAs and temples;

2. An understanding of the family hierarchical structure, the importance of respecting authority, the influence of the leaders and the requesting of their assistance;

3. The use of ethnically similar workers in providing direct services;

4. The understanding and acceptance of the ways in which problems are expressed through psychosomatic symptoms; and

5. The exploration of the individual's concept of mental illness and mental health, as well as her or his expectations about the services.

## Implications for Training and Research

Educators and trainers need to be familiar with Buddhism as a belief system and a practical teaching of social conduct. Buddhism departs from Western theory in that it does not focus on eliminating or changing the unhappiness, the undesirable, the negative; rather, the goal is to acknowledge a problem's existence and understand its true nature. Research on the contributions of Buddhism to human services is practically nonexistent. One of the benefits of exploring Buddhist concepts and social conduct

is that such efforts will provide valuable knowledge to Western mental health practitioners during this time of social unrest.

## References

Ajahn Chah. (1982). *Bodhinyana: A collection of Dhamma talks*. Bangkok, Thailand: Bung Wai Forest Monastery.

Buddhadasa Bhikkhu. (1988). *Handbook for mankind*. Bangkok, Thailand: Supanit Press.

Canda, E. R., & Phaobtong, T. (1992). Buddhism as a support system for Southeast Asian refugees. *Social Work, 37*, 61-67.

Jayatilleke, K. N. (1987). *Aspects of Buddhist social philosophy*. Chiangmai, Thailand: The Buddhist Publication Foundation.

Nguyen, L. D. (1984, March). Indochinese cross-cultural adjustment and communication. Paper presented at the annual meeting of the Teachers of English to Speakers of Other Languages, Houston, TX.

Owen, T. C. (1985). *Southeast Asian mental health*. Washington, DC: National Institute of Mental Health.

Plamintr, S. (1994). *Getting to know Buddhism*. Bangkok, Thailand: Buddhadhamma Foundation.

Ratanasuwan, P. (1972). *Mental health and religion*. Bangkok, Thailand: Home of Psychical Research.

# Counseling Children of Cultural and Diversity Orientation

*Beverly A. Snyder*

## Overview

As few as about three percent of Americans can claim to be true natives (Eskimos, Hawaiians, Aleutian Islanders, and American Indians). The rest of us originated somewhere else and immigrated here. Estimates are that in the next five years, more than a third of our children will be from an ethnic minority (Sue, 1981). These children form a cultural group characterized by certain assumptions: they may not be as verbal as adults, their sense of time is more immediate, and they are less likely to refer themselves for counseling. The increase in ethnic minority children challenges counselors to find appropriate resources for meeting the needs presented by this population.

## Special Problems Children Face

Children whose cultural and linguistic backgrounds are different from that of the dominant culture do not yet have complete access to the full range of social services. Issues include the following:

1. only one third of limited-English-proficient children receive any help for their linguistic needs;
2. the drop-out rate for minority children is higher than that of any other group; and
3. those who provides services for children often lack meaningful multi-cultural education (Snyder, 1994).

Pedersen and Carey (1994) note that children receive a great deal of pressure from their families to succeed in school and the world because these children may well be the first family members to matriculate through the American school system. The child is caught in the middle, between parents who believe that the child represents their family honor and pride, and the school, which values independence and autonomy.

Children frequently face adults who perpetuate a view that minorities are culturally "disadvantaged," "deficient," or "deprived," because these minorities lack many of the advantages of mainstream children (books, toys, language, etc., Atkinson, Morten, & Sue, 1993). This exacerbates feelings among children that they are somehow damaged because of their cultural values, families, or life-styles.

Another issue is the culture-bound values that are used to judge normality and abnormality in children. These serve to hinder and distort communication that may already be problematical for those children who do not speak and use English well. Existing in an unfamiliar place between the expectations of home and the world of mainstream society creates additional stress and anxiety. These children lack the familiar signposts along the way that indicate they are on the right track and doing what is normal and typical for their age group.

## Belief System and World View

Locke (1995) notes that children of diversity exist in two cultures—that of their cultural heritage and that of the dominant culture. Many aspects of their cultural origins stay with them and serve to support their survival. "These include dialect, folklore, adult-child relationships, family structure, music, generosity,...respect" and religious practices and beliefs (Locke, 1995, p. 22). These cultural components need to be recognized and incorporated in any work done with children.

Many scholars (Lee, 1995; Sue, 1981) have described core characteristics of diverse cultures. While the following are not culturally specific, they are general guidelines to use in working with children and they offer counselors practical suggestions. Counselors should use:

1. Approaches that are culturally sensitive and relevant,
2. Consideration of their learning styles (often visual and kinesthetic),
3. Communication patterns that are altered to increase the involvement of children in the learning process, and
4. understanding that they:
   (a) Respond in right-brained terms (whole versus parts)
   (b) Prefer inferential reasoning and approximations
   (c) Prefer to focus on people rather than things
   (d) Tend to have a keen sense of justice
   (e) Lean toward a concern for others
   (f) Prefer novelty and personal distinctiveness
   (g) Are proficient in non-verbal communication.

In sum, children's belief system and world view represent a unique blend of their families' values and the characteristics that describe the mainstream culture.

### Successful Programs

With the rise of school developmental guidance programs children of diversity have been receiving more viable interventions (Snyder, 1994). A fundamental concept is that such services promote human development through counseling, coordination of programs, and consultation with all concerned. The developmental theory base suggests that counseling professionals are challenged to help young people negotiate the various developmental tasks that are valid for all cultures, not just the White mainstream.

Successful programs and services take into consideration the uniqueness of children of diversity. These children are interdependent, fatalistic (nature is stronger than man), not inclined to change, and they favor tradition and a well understood hierarchical social structure that determines opportunities. Families are more important than the individual and there is an orientation to the past. Children follow group consensus and tend to endure whatever comes their way. Discipline is affectively based and teachers and counselors are seen as authority figures. Extracurricular activities are not encouraged (Snyder, 1994).

### Implications

Service delivery must address the diverse cultural needs of the children who are served. Interventions must be culturally relevant and should focus on highly personalized relationships in which sharing and values play a large part. The counselor must take an active leadership role when working with children of diversity. For example, children expect counselors to determine the issues to be worked on and in which order people should speak.

Counselors must consider the communication styles of children, being sensitive to the importance of silence and nonverbal communication, recognize the dependent roles and family dynamics that place father as patriarch and mother as nurturer and caretaker. Effective counselors utilize informal support systems such as churches, ethnic clubs, and family associations. Additionally, they attempt to strengthen the family unit and to acknowledge the child's need to function in two different worlds at the sametime.

School counselors and play therapists are challenged to recognize the impact the environment has on the child's adjustment to mainstream culture. Shade notes in Pedersen's 1990 text that the environment should be moderately arousing, pleasant, have sufficient information to be stimulating, and arranged to allow easy movement.

Interactional style must be recognized as often having more importance to the child than learning a task. Children need frequent attention and reinforcement regarding their completion of a task as expected and they enjoy being held in high regard by the teacher or counselor. Placing children in cooperative groups is an effective strategy for children with sociocentric learning styles.

## Case Study

Enrico is a seven year old who was referred to the school counselor because of an inability to sit still and complete assignments. His nuclear family includes five brothers and sisters, his mother who does not work outside the home, and his father who runs a corner food store in the neighborhood. A happy, free-flowing chaos describes Enrico's home in which the television is on, children run and play, and mother is heard singing. The counselor learns that Enrico's teacher does not provide frequent feedback and interpersonal warmth but rather focuses on tasks and strict organization. Eventually Enrico is transferred to another teacher whose style more closely matches his and whose classroom is less structured and more interactive. He is placed in a cooperative learning group with other students with whom he can interact. Within weeks Enrico is once again cooperative and completing his work.

The description of Enrico's home life indicates the cultural milieu in which he has been raised and provides a clue to his present difficulties. The counselor discovers that the classroom environment does not support his learning style and is very diifferent from the life-style in which he was raised. The intervention of transferring Enrico to a classroom which more closely matches his interactive and learning style is based both on cultural awareness and the knowledge base which supports the special problems minority children face.

## References

Atkinson, D. R., Morten, G., & Sue, D. W. (1993). *Counseling American minorities.* Dubuque, IA: Brown & Benchmark.

Lee, C. C. (Ed.). (1995). *Counseling for diversity: A guide for school counselors and related professionals.* Needham Heights, MA: Allyn and Bacon.

Locke, D. C. (1995). Counseling interventions with African American youth. In C. C. Lee (Ed.), *Counseling for diversity: A guide for school counselors and related professionals* (pp. 21-40). Needham Heights, MA: Allyn and Bacon.

Pedersen, P., & Carey, J. C. (1994). *Multicultural counseling in schools.* Needham Heights, MA: Allyn and Bacon.

Pedersen, P., Locke, D. C., Shade, B., & Parker, L. D. (1990). *A culturally diverse world.* (ERIC Document Reproduction Service No. CG 022 263)

Snyder, B. A. (1994). *Multiculturalism in the classroom.* Kearney, NE: University of Nebraska at Kearney.

Sue, D. W. (1981). *Counseling the culturally different: Theory and practice.* New York: John Wiley & Sons.

# Culture, Diversity, And Disability

*Catherine Marshall*

## Overview

Lee (1991) noted that "as the United States prepares to enter a new century, a new counseling professional must emerge—one who has a solid knowledge base with which to meet the challenges of counseling practice with culturally diverse client groups" (p. 213). For the past 15 years, research documenting the need for different service delivery approaches, as regards minority and diverse populations, has been readily available to the counseling profession (e.g., Atkins, 1982; Marshall, Johnson, Martin, Saravanabhavan, & Bradford, 1992; Wright & Emener, 1989). Researchers and counselor educators have provided specific guidance on how best to work with culturally diverse populations (see, e.g., Acosta, Yamamoto, & Evans, 1982; Atkinson, Morten, & Wing Sue, 1989; Marshall, Johnson, & Lonetree, 1993; Pedersen, 1988; Wright, 1988).

However, it would appear that counseling professionals have resisted those changes in preservice education and service delivery that would facilitate meeting the needs of ethnic minority persons who have disabilities. The following discussion presents:

1. challenges facing counselors and counselor educators in regard to more adequately serving such individuals,
2. advances which have been made in the field, and
3. recommendations for professionals concerned with improving the quality and appropriateness of counseling services available to culturally diverse persons who have disabilities.

## Challenges

Even where well-intentioned professionals have recognized the importance of culture in counseling, positive associations with diversity, as well as specific requirements for obtaining and evaluating cultural competence, are too often lacking. Additionally, the specific needs of persons associated with a subpopulation, or minorities within a given culturally-diverse group, are too often ignored. For example, how do the various Asian cultures view a person with a disability, in contrast to Anglo cultures? What counseling implications for the individual with a disability might the cultural "messages" associated with disability have? Is a counseling approach that focuses on the needs of an individual appropriate, given a person with a disability from a collectivist society such as with many indigenous cultures?

## Professional Counselors

University and college counseling centers include some of the following accreditation standards: "Staff should have the necessary training and diversity to meet the needs of students of varying ethnic and cultural backgrounds, children of dysfunctional families, victims of sexual and physical abuse, and students with educational deficiencies" (Kiracofe, et al., 1994, pp. 39, 41)." Interestingly, different "cultural backgrounds" is linked, even if unintentionally, with negative experiences such as "dysfunctional families," "sexual and physical abuse," and "educational deficiencies." Further, while the accreditation standards require that "professional staff must have had appropriate course work at the graduate level" in content areas such as theories of personality and abnormal psychology, "necessary training" as regards cultural competencies are not specified. Thus, while the accreditation standards indicate some awareness of the needs of culturally different students, ethnic minority students, as well as ethnic minority students with disabilities, may find that the university-based counselor is not fully prepared to meet their counseling needs.

## Specialized Training in Rehabilitation Counseling

Counselors particularly interested in serving persons with disabilities may prepare for this role by specializing in the profession of rehabilitation counseling. Dodd, Nelson, Ostwald, and Fischer (1991) surveyed "postsecondary education programs that offer the masters degree in rehabilitation counseling" (p. 47). While 45 programs were identified, only 20 respondents, representing less than half of the existing programs, reported having a "multicultural component" (p. 47). Concerning the need for rehabilitation counselors to receive multicultural training, Fischer (1991) noted that "overcoming cross-cultural counseling barriers requires understanding the consumer's cultural attitudes toward both counselors and counseling process..." (p. 43).

As with accreditation standards for university and college counseling centers, the accreditation body for rehabilitation counselor education programs, the Council of Rehabilitation Education (CORE), does not specify, or specifically require, counseling course work related to cultural diversity. The CORE accreditation manual reads, "the required curriculum of graduate study . . . would typically include . . . multi-cultural and gender issues" ("Council," 1994, p. 15). While *educational outcomes* such as "the ability to demonstrate knowledge of the history, philosophy, and legislation affecting rehabilitation" (p. 17) are specified, no cultural competency outcomes specifically related to counseling skills are delineated.

## Advances

As stated earlier, preservice counselor educators have not demonstrated strong leadership in training counselors to meet the needs of persons with disabilities from diverse cultures. Even so, a wealth of information exists for developing the necessary course work. For example, Wing Sue (1992) has identified racism as an issue that may be difficult for the counselor to face, but which should be addressed within a counselor-in-training supportive environment. According to Wing Sue, "counselors must realize that the world views of minority groups may be strongly influenced by experiences of racism and discrimination. Minority clients oftentimes enter counseling with a healthy suspicion of the counselor, the counseling process, and the institutions in which the process is embedded" (p. 13). He stressed that questions reflecting this suspicion "should not be viewed as pathological, but as a healthy, functional mechanism used by the culturally different to survive in an oppressive environment" (p. 13).

Specifically, as regards persons who have disabilities, a leader in the field of rehabilitation counseling has suggested that with the changing demography of the United States, as documented by the 1990 U.S. Census, new models of counseling for persons with disabilities may need to be developed (Leung, 1993). Leung observed that "with changes in clientele, different models may need to be explored.., and that recognition not only of the roles of family members, but also their importance in issues such as the motivation for rehabilitation, may be important..." (p. 9). Similarly, Fischer (1991) concluded that "service delivery systems which reflect the dominant culture must be made accessible to the consumer in order for the goals of rehabilitation to be achieved" (p. 43).

## Case Study

One example of the need for both a new model of counseling, as well as an accessible service delivery system, involves a Native family interviewed by the author as part of research conducted with the Eastern Band of Cherokee Indians (Marshall, & Cerveny, 1994).

Mr. and Mrs. J. are the elderly parents of a middle-aged son. The son, who has both mental retardation and mental illness, received services through the public vocational rehabilitation agency and subsequently obtained a job. The parents, while pleased that the son was gainfully employed, reported having had great difficulty dealing with years of abusive behavior from their son. In an attempt to be positive, Mrs. J. stated, "But, he only threatened to shoot me once." Mr. and Mrs. J. reported that because they were concerned their son might harm their grandchildren for whom they also provide care, they began the process of securing for their son his own home; he now lives "independently." The son lives in his own house that was built on the property of Mr. and Mrs. J. and within a few yards of their home. Mr. and Mrs. J. provide their son with emotional and social support, but report an improved quality of life since he no longer lives with them. Mr. J. stated that he and Mrs. J. have never know how best to work with their son—in over 20 years they have never been approached by any service agency and they have never asked for assistance for themselves. However, Mr. J. stated that he would welcome "visitation" by service providers and information on how to control his son's abusive behavior.

The case of Mr. and Mrs. J. demonstrates how the majority-culture service system often fails American Indian families. Counselors typically wait in an office until approached by the individual client who is asking for services. Counselors should understand that while supportive families may be reluctant to ask for help, they may both need and welcome assistance. A service delivery system that assumes the existence of a supportive family network, and assumes the responsibility to be accessible through respectful outreach, would be more appropriate for American Indians than our current system.

### Recommendations

According to Wing Sue (1992), "doing the right thing—embracing multiculturalism—is not easy. Yet it is the only viable option we have.... We can no longer afford to treat multiculturalism as an ancillary, rather than an integral, part of counseling" (p. 14). To assist counselors in better serving culturally diverse persons who have disabilities, the following recommendations are made:

1. Begin training now. While professional counselor training programs would, ideally, require specific course work in meeting the specific counseling needs of culturally diverse persons with disabilities, and while we must continue to work toward having all counselor accreditation bodies recognize, support, and delineate in their regulations the specific skills needed by culturally competent counselors who would serve persons with disabilities, individual counselors can take responsibility for initiating their own professional development by seeking out training related to counseling persons from diverse populations, including persons from different cultures who have disabilities. Self-assessment and self-training might begin by becoming familiar with the current literature available (see, e.g., Makas, Marshall, & Wehman, in press; Wright & Leung, 1992).

2. Avoid simplistic solutions. One counselor recently stated to the author, "We are doing a good job in the area of diversity—we have black counselors working with black clients and white counselors working with white clients." How do such solutions differ from racist segregation practices?

3. Avoid denying the relevance of cultural diversity. One administrator of a public agency that provides rehabilitation counseling services recently stated to the author, "We do not acknowledge ethnicity and we think that is the way it should be."

4. Open a dialogue. Who should determine the curricula/training agendas in regard to appropriate counseling with culturally diverse persons who have disabilities? Should it be people with disabilities of the majority culture who subscribe to the values of an individualistic society? Can such individuals be open to the values of people with disabilities from collectivist societies? Can we work together to share what we know about culture and disability—not only on a domestic front but also on an international basis?

5. Learn from successful and experienced programs. Effective programs, both in rural and urban areas, are meeting the needs of culturally diverse persons who have disabilities. Counseling professionals responsible for developing curricula/ training agendas should budget resources for consultants from such programs—programs such as tribally-controlled rehabilitation programs that assist American Indians with disabilities through a range of interventions, including traditional Native healing ceremonies and forms of work/productivity in-line with local economies and the Native culture.

### References

Acosta, F. X., Yamamoto, J., & Evans, L. A. (1982). *Effective psychotherapy for low-income and minority patients.* New York: Plenum Press.

Atkins, B. J. (1982). Women as members of special populations in rehabilitation. In L. G. Perlman, & K. C. Arneson (Eds.), *Women and rehabilitation of disabled persons.* Alexandria, VA: The National Rehabilitation Association.

Atkinson, D. R., Morten, G., & Wing Sue, D. (1989). *Counseling American minorities: A cross-cultural perspective* (3rd ed.). Dubuque, IA: William C. Brown.

Council on Rehabilitation Education, Inc. (1994). *Accreditation manual for rehabilitation counselor education programs.* (Available from CORE; 1835 Rohlwing Road, Suite E; Rolling Meadows, Illinois 60008)

Dodd, J. M., Nelson, J. R., Ostwald, S. W., & Fischer, J. (1991). Rehabilitation counselor education programs' response to cultural pluralism. *Journal of Applied Rehabilitation Counseling, 22* (1), 46-48.

Fischer, J. M. (1991). A comparison between American Indian and non-Indian consumers of vocational rehabilitation services. *Journal of Applied Rehabilitation Counseling, 22* (1), 43-45.

Kiracofe, N. M., Donn, P. A., Grant, C. O., Podolnick, E. E., Bingham, R. P., Bolland, H. R., Carney, C. G. Clementson, J., Gallagher, R. P., Grosz, R. D., Handy, L., Hansche, J. H., Mack, J. K., Sanz, D., Walker, L. J., & Yamada, K. T. (1994). Accreditation standards for university and college counseling centers. *Journal of Counseling & Development, 73,* 38-43.

Lee, C. C. (1991). New approaches to diversity: Implications for multicultural counselor training and research. In C. C. Lee & B. L. Richardson (Eds.), *Multicultural issues in counseling: New approaches to diversity* (pp. 209-214). Alexandria, VA: American Association of Counseling and Development.

Leung, P. (1993). A changing demography and its challenge. *Journal of Vocational Rehabilitation, 3* (1), 3-11.

Makas, E., Marshall, C. A., & Wehman, P. (in press). Cultural diversity and disability: Developing respect for differences. In P. Wehman (Ed.), *Exceptional individuals in school, community and work.* Austin, TX: PRO-ED.

Marshall, C. A., & Cerveny, L. (1994). *American Indian family support systems and implications for the rehabilitation process: The Eastern Band of Cherokee Indians and the Mississippi Band of Choctaw Indians. Final Report.* Flagstaff: Northern Arizona University, Institute for Human Development, Arizona University Affiliated Program, American Indian Rehabilitation Research and Training Center. (Available from the American Indian Rehabilitation Research and Training Center, Institute for Human Development, Northern Arizona University, PO Box 5630, Flagstaff, AZ 86011)

Marshall, C. A., Johnson, M. J., Martin, W. E. Jr., Saravanabhavan, R. C., & Bradford, B. (1992). The rehabilitation needs of American Indians with disabilities in an urban setting. *Journal of Rehabilitation, 58* (2) 13-21.

Marshall, C. A., Johnson, S. R., & Lonetree, G. L. (1993). Acknowledging our diversity: Vocational rehabilitation and American Indians. *Journal of Vocational Rehabilitation, 3*(1), 12-19.

Pedersen, P. (1988). *The triad model of multicultural counselor training: A handbook for developing multicultural awareness.* Alexandria, VA: American Association for Counseling and Development.

Wing Sue, D. (1992). The challenge of multiculturalism: The road less traveled. *American Counselor, 1* (1), 6-14.

Wright, T. J. (1988). Enhancing the professional preparation of rehabilitation counselors for improved services to ethnic minorites with disabilities. *The Journal of Applied Rehabilitation Counseling, 19,* 4-10.

Wright, T. J., & Emener, W. G. (Eds.). (1989). *Ethnic minorities with disabilities: An annotated bibliography of rehabilitation literature.* (Available from the Department of Rehabilitation Counseling, University of South Florida, Tampa, FL, 33620)

Wright, T. J., & Leung, P. (Eds.). (1992). *The unique needs of minorities with disabilities: Setting an agenda for the future.* Conference proceedings. (Available from the National Clearing House of Rehabilitation Training Materials; 816 West 6th Street; OSU; Stillwater, OK 74078)

# Chapter 19

# Economic Status and Mental Health

*Raymond P. Lorion*
*Cheryl C. Holland*
*Tracy Myers*

## Overview

Mental health scientists and service providers have long studied the relationships among socioeconomic status (SES), the prevalence of emotional disorders, and the effectiveness of therapeutic interventions. Similar relationships are found for SES and physical disorders. Less recognized is the cultural quality of SES's influence on language patterns, residential, occupational and recreational options and expectations, and social network and resources. In addition to race and ethnicity, SES shapes significantly who one is and what one does. Understandably then, SES is important as an aggregate index of individual economic resources, social status, and social influence.

That aggregation has salience for interactions between mental health researchers/service providers and their subjects and clients. In the past, methodologists controlled SES as a potential confound in studies of etiological processes, intervention mechanisms, and intervention effects. Increasingly appreciated, however, is SES's influence on normative and pathological development and on treatment processes and outcomes. It is hoped that recognition of that influence will catalyze new research activity, as well as sensitize service providers in considering SES-related information as salient to treatment selection and conduct.

## Defining and Measuring SES

Conceptualizing and measuring SES is highly complex. As noted, the construct, SES, refers to sociological factors (e.g., status, class); demographic factors (e.g., age, race, gender); economic factors (e.g., income, eligibility for public assistance); and psychological factors (e.g., self-efficacy, empowerment). The Index of Social Position (ISP), for example, was used by Hollingshead and Redlich (1958) in their epidemiological survey of mental health services use in New Haven. Based on a respondent's (or the head of the respondent's household) occupation and education, five levels of social standing were defined. Although nearly forty years old, the ISP (with some modification to reflect a spouse's education and occupation) remains in use. A comparable approach was applied by Srole, Langner, Michael, Opler and Rennie (1962) in their study of Manhattan residents' mental health needs. In this instance, family SES was defined in terms of father's education, occupation, total family income, and housing costs. Continued use of either the ISP or Srole measures should be questioned given the diversity of family structures in contemporary society (e.g., dual vs. single parents; mother-alone headed households; merged family households, etc.) and the increasing dissociation between occupation and income.

Alternatives are available. The occupational status of all adults contributing to a household's income, for example, can be rated and aggregated (e.g., Nakao and Treas, 1992). Social area and census tract information of one's residence, reports of overall family income, or eligibility for school-based subsidized lunch programs have served as proxies of individual SES, especially in studies of the mental health status of youth (Lorion & Felner, 1986).

Two widely accepted assumptions about SES have recently been challenged. If validated, these challenges are likely to redefine the measurement and interpretation of SES. Mental health scientists/service providers have long assumed that SES is most salient for those with limited economic and societal resources. By contrast, Adler, et al.,

(1994) have demonstrated *for physical health* a gradient effect *across the entire SES range.* Although little is known about the effects of SES at the upper income ranges, Adler et al. argue that such a gradient effect makes sense given SES's link with characteristics of one's physical, occupational, social, economic, and health opportunities. Adler et al. found that *within* any SES level, relative rather than absolute status relates significantly to the nature and effects on physical health. The mental health disciplines must determine if and how this gradient effect influences emotional functioning.

Featherman, Spenner, and Tsunematsu (1988) challenge the assumption that SES is an invariant characteristic. Focusing on childhood, Featherman et al. found that many youth, especially those born into the lower SES ranges, experience a succession of SES changes. These shifts reflect changes in parent(s)' educational, occupational, marital, and residential status. Clearly, such changes occur not only to youth but also to their families. As yet unknown are the implications of SES shifts for parents' attitudes and parenting behaviors, self-esteem, capacity for stress management, etc. which, in turn, influence the mental health of youth. Also unknown are the implications of such shifts for adults' vulnerability to emotional disorder, and willingness to seek and respond to mental health interventions.

### SES and Mental Health Needs and Services

The links between SES and the prevalence of emotional and behavioral disorders are well established. Widely cited evidence of this link, from Hollingshead and Redlich (1958) to Srole et al. (1962), has repeatedly been confirmed and has informed mental health services for low SES clients (Garfield, 1994; Lorion & Felner, 1986). Unlike SES, gender, race, and age do not relate independently to levels of disorder or treatment responsiveness. Although women, members of minority groups, children, and the elderly are overrepresented in the lowest SES groups, their measured levels of disorder appear primarily to reflect access to economic and societal resources. Epidemiological data document levels of disorder across segments of the population. They do not, however, explain causally the variation in prevalence across SES levels. Lorion and Felner (1986) argue that available empirical, observational, and clinical evidence supports the conclusion that poverty and its associated limits on economic, societal, and remedial resources are etiologically significant for understanding this link. Adler et al. (1994) argue, that one's relative economic position has significant and broad implications for where and how one lives, for experienced stresses, and for available resources.

Ironically, service providers often make assumptions about a client's SES with little direct information. Although not, to our knowledge, systematically studied, clients probably have even less objective information about the past or current SES of their service provider. That omission is important given evidence that the provider's SES background relates significantly to treatment duration and outcome (Lorion & Felner, 1986). Negative associations are reported between SES and responsiveness to psychotherapy. Those most in need of services have traditionally had least access to them, have been most likely to terminate prematurely, and have been least served by traditional interventions (Garfield, 1994; Lorion & Felner, 1986). It should be noted, however, that these conclusions reflect findings obtained when long-term interventions were predominantly used and when service providers were primarily middle-class, white males. Interventions sensitive to low-SES experiences, needs, and interactional styles significantly increase treatment success (Garfield, 1994; Lorion & Felner, 1986). Of particular import is the use of time-limited modalities that are culturally-sensitive interventions which also meet the crisis elements of client needs.

### The Breadth of the SES Effect

To unravel the relationships among SES, researchers must appreciate the fact that the influence of SES extends beyond the client to the researcher, the service provider, the service systems, and their interactions. Assumptions about SES of *all* who participate in mental health research and service, both directly and indirectly, sways the outcomes of that participation. That such assumptions seem quite malleable gives promise to the potential for altering described SES health linkages. Therapists respond quite positively, for example, to training which sensitizes them to the perspectives and experiences of clients from diverse economic and cultural backgrounds. Similarly, the completion and effectiveness of mental health interventions increases after clients participate in brief orientations to the nature of the therapeutic process. Zane, Hatanaka, Park, and Akutsu (1994) provide important evidence of the capacity to influence positive treatment outcomes when issues of cultural sensitivity are addressed for both the service provider and the client.

## Conclusion

SES remains a salient issue for mental health research and service in the coming decades. Those providing mental health services must be aware of evidence linking SES with the prevalence of disorder, client responsiveness to treatment, and therapist effectiveness. Importantly, understanding SES has become more complicated of late. Assumptions about the invariance of SES status and about its importance only for those from the lowest SES groups have been strongly challenged. These challenges argue for therapists to learn as much as possible about each client's SES and the associated cultural context. The pervasive influence of SES also demands that the therapist recognize personal biases attached to various SES levels, experiences, and life styles. In a very real sense, SES is one contributor to therapeutic success which can be positively shaped through understanding and sensitivity.

## References

Adler, N. E., Boyce, T., Chesney, M. A., Cohen, S., Folkman, S., Kahn, R. L. & Syme, S. L. (1994). Socioeconomic status and health: The challenge of the gradient. *American Psychologist, 49*, 15-24.

Featherman, D. L., Spenner, K. I., & Tsunematsu, N. (1988). Class and the socialization of children: Constancy, change, or irrelevance? In M. Hetherington, R. Lerner, & F. Perlmutter (Eds.), *Child development: A life-span perspective* (pp. 67-89). Hillsdale, NJ: Lawrence Erlbaum Associates, Inc.

Garfield, S. L. (1994). Research on client variables in psychotherapy. In A. E. Bergin & S. L. Garfield (Eds.), *Handbook of psychotherapy and behavior change* (4th ed., pp. 190-228). New York: John Wiley & Sons, Inc.

Hollingshead, A. B., & Redlich, F. C. (1958). *Social class and mental illness*. New York: Wiley.

Lorion, R. P., & Felner, R. D. (1986). Research on psychotherapy with the disadvantaged. In S. L. Garfield & A. E. Bergin (Eds.), *Handbook of psychotherapy and behavior change* (3rd ed., pp. 739-775). New York: Wiley.

Nakao, K., & Treas, J. (1992). The 1989 socioeconomic Index of Occupations: Construction from the 1989 Occupational Prestige Scores. *General Social Survey Methodological Report No. 74*. NORC, University of Chicago.

Srole, L., Langer, T. S., Michael, S. T., Opler, M. K., & Rennie, T. A. C. (1962). *Mental health in the metropolis: The midtown Manhattan Study*. New York: McGraw-Hill.

Zane, N., Hatanaka, H., Park, S., & Akutsu, P. (1994). Ethnic-specific mental health services: Evaluation of the parallel approach for Asian-American clients. *Journal of Community Psychology, 22*, 68-81.

# Counseling the HIV-infected Client

*Kathryn L. Norsworthy*
*Eva Fajardo*

### Overview

Acquired immune deficiency syndrome (AIDS) has become a household word in the 1990's. This collection of diseases and conditions occurs when an individual is infected with human immunodeficiency virus (HIV), a virus that leads to the severe compromising of the body's immune system. As the immune system weakens, the infected individual becomes susceptible to a range of opportunistic infections, and, eventually, most HIV-infected persons die from a major AIDS-related illness. While the causes of AIDS are still uncertain, it is generally agreed in the scientific community that HIV is carried in blood, semen, vaginal fluids, and mother's milk, and is transmitted via heterosexual intercourse, anal-penile penetration, sharing used needles, blood transfusion, and other contexts in which infected fluids from one individual enter the blood stream of another (Winiarski, 1991).

Statistics from the Centers for Disease Control reveal over 388,000 reported cases of AIDS in the United States to date (Centers for Disease Control, 1994). Early in the pandemic, gay men and IV drug users were hardest hit, but today, no age, gender, class, sexual orientation, or racial/ethnic group has been left unaffected.

Although HIV-infected individuals represent diverse backgrounds, common issues sometimes bring them together at various stages of their disease process. This "cultural identity" as a Person With AIDS (PWA) is often linked with political activism, the seeking of mental health and medical services, and public education efforts. Thus, it is useful to conceptualize counseling issues that are common to this special population. Still, it must be noted that the person is not the disease, and that the multitude of other individual and cultural aspects of each PWA defines him/her. Additionally, women, persons of color, and indigent persons with HIV disease continue to be disenfranchised from the "AIDS community," reflective of continuing societal oppression and the lack of understanding of their needs.

Much information has surfaced in the literature about the special counseling issues of the HIV-infected client (Hoffman, 1991; Winniarski, 1991). Common themes include the following:

1. *Social stigma.* Society, in its hysteria, has responded to the PWA by victim-blaming, criticism, and outright exclusion, often leading the infected person to feel "tainted" or undeserving of physical contact with another human being.

2. *Existential concerns.* A shortened lifespan leads to questions about the meaning of HIV, purpose of life, how to live and die in a meaningful way, and suicide. Spirituality often becomes important as a source of meaning, strength, and comfort.

3. *Health and medical concerns.* Many of the drugs and treatment regimens are experimental or do not have convincing data regarding their effects. A sizable proportion of clients educate themselves and become very involved in decision-making regarding their medical treatment. Due to the uncertainty and unpredictability of the course of AIDS, infected individuals may be hypervigilant to any physical symptoms, common colds, or other such conditions, fearing the beginning of a major AIDS-related illness. Limited availability of informed physicians who are willing to treat this population is a reality. Due to the costly nature of prophylaxis and treatment of AIDS-related conditions, appropriate medical services may be unaffordable, especially in later stages of the disease when financial resources have been depleted.

4. *Sexuality.* Safer sex practices, how to inform a potential sexual partner about one's HIV status, and creative ways to enjoy sex are on the

minds of many individuals in counseling.

5. *Loss and grief.* The most obvious loss is the loss of wellness—the erosion of physical and mental functioning. Most persons with HIV experience loss of financial resources and vocational identity. Loss of social and family support may also occur.

Important to mention are some of the special issues particular to subgroups infected with HIV. Dilley, Pies, and Helquist (1993) provide an in-depth look at the following diversity issues in their volume, *Face to Face: A Guide to AIDS Counseling.*

Gay men encounter significant homophobia in tandem with an already critical society. Many of these men find themselves in the position of telling their families and friends that they are HIV-infected and are "coming out" about their sexual orientations. Additionally, because the gay community was so hard hit by AIDS, gay men typically have lost significant numbers from their friendship networks and communities to this disease.

Women, the invisible, yet ever growing group, present a number of special considerations. In addition to encountering societal sexism in the form of pressure to continue to take care of everyone else before herself, the HIV-infected woman is faced with the fact that most AIDS-related research is done with male subjects. Likewise, as the designated caretaker of children in this society, a woman must continuously balance her own needs with those of her children and family. Childbearing is also affected since the virus can be transmitted from mother to unborn child, and during the process of breastfeeding. See Rieder and Ruppelt's (1988) excellent book, *AIDS: The Women*, for a more complete review of this topic.

A dual diagnosis of HIV-infection and drug or alcohol dependence brings further challenges to the counseling arena. Questions of whether or not to treat an individual who is actively using, how to intervene when drug/alcohol treatment is needed, all in the face of a society that has generally judged this population to be unworthy of saving, come to the fore. Here we often find homeless and disenfranchised individuals who may have mental illness or other severe

psychopathology.

Class and socioeconomic status of the HIV-infected client mediate many aspects of the individual's life. Whether to offer support in meeting basic needs, what kind of language to use in therapy, locus of control and responsibility issues, and the like may all be impacted by this important variable.

Since a broad range of ethnic groups have been infected by HIV, it would be worthwhile to understand the cultural factors that might interact with the previously discussed counseling concerns. Family structure, values regarding sexuality, gender roles within the culture, basic world view, and response of the cultural group to AIDS are examples of areas of investigation for the culturally sensitive counselor.

Early in the pandemic, largely through the efforts of the gay/lesbian/bisexual community, AIDS Service Organizations (ASO's) were established (Barouch, 1992). These successful organizations are open to all persons infected or affected by the HIV virus. Services provided by ASO's may include case management, housing, peer support groups, psychological and medical services or referrals, social networking, food banks, condom distribution, financial support, education, fund-raising, grant writing, community relations and transportation. However, in spite of the efforts that have been made on behalf of HIV-infected individuals, health and social services reform aimed at increased access to services is needed, as are federal and state funding sources for continued AIDS programming.

Working with the HIV-infected person and his/her loved ones presents special challenges to the counselor. Most counselors are affected by clients facing the dying process or substantial losses in physical and psychological functioning. The counselor may begin to experience his/her own existential/spiritual dilemmas. As clients die, grief and bereavement may become paramount for the counselor working with persons with AIDS. On a different note, any prejudices, such as homophobia, heterosexism, AIDS stigmatizing, racism, classism, or sexism are bound to surface when working with HIV-infected clients. Thus, the responsible counselor must continuously engage in self-care, self exploration, and limits-setting in order to effectively avoid burn-out and to set proper boundaries in the client-counselor relationship.

Legal/ethical issues must be mentioned in working with HIV-infected individuals (Wood, Marks, & Dilley, 1990). For example, counselors are faced with clients who want to discuss suicide as an option if they become very ill or begin to experience severe physical suffering. Some clients continue to have unprotected sexual contact after infection, or choose not to tell a partner about their HIV status. These counseling issues challenge mental health providers to balance client confidentiality and choice with legal responsibilities such as duty to warn or duty to protect.

Substantial research is needed to validate effective counseling and prevention strategies for the diverse range of individuals infected with the HIV virus. Most counselor education programs do not include in-depth education in counseling HIV-infected clients, though recently, outside organizations have begun to provide free-standing institutes to address mental health training needs.

### Case Study

Estelle is a 38 year old mother of two children, ages 13 and 8. She was infected with HIV five years ago through heterosexual sexual contact with a boyfriend who used IV drugs. She has just come home from the hospital after recovering from her first opportunistic infection, pneumocystis carini pneumonia, and has just recognized that she will almost certainly die before her children grow to adulthood. She tells the counselor that she is very frightened of what will happen to her children as she has no close living relatives, and that she is terrified of the suffering she has seen many people with AIDS in her support group experience during their final days. Further, the drugs she is taking seem to be causing excess bleeding between periods, and Estelle cannot get any clear answers from her doctors about this issue. She states, "I need help planning for this last phase of my life."

Estelle's story clearly illustrates the emergence of HIV as a dominant theme in her life requiring that the counselor have specific knowledge about the medical aspects of the disease's progression and its corresponding psychological impact. We can also see that her gender, class, developmental, and familial status also intricately interact with her AIDS related issues, demanding both cultural counseling sensitivity and competence.

### References

Barouch, G. (1992). *Support groups: The human face of the HIV/AIDS epidemic.* Huntington Station, New York: Long Island Association for AIDS Care, Inc.

Centers for Disease Control. (1994). HIV/AIDS surveillance report, *6* (1), 1-22.

Dilley, J. W., Pies, C., & Helquist, M. (Eds.). (1993). *Face to face: A guide to AIDS counseling.* San Francisco: AIDS Health Project.

Hoffman, M. A. (1991). Counseling the HIV-infected client: A psychosocial model for assessment and intervention. *The Counseling Psychologist, 19,* 467-542.

Rieder, I. & Ruppelt, P. (Eds.). (1988). *AIDS: The women.* San Francisco: Cleis Press.

Winiarski, M. G. (1991). *AIDS-related psychotherapy.* Elmsford, NY: Pergamon.

Wood, G. J., Marks, R., & Dilley, J. W. (1990). *AIDS law for mental health professionals.* San Francisco: AIDS Health Project.

# The Impact of Homelessness on Children and Their Families

*Judy Daniels*

One of the fastest growing segments of the homeless population is families with children. Several factors have contributed to the rapid increase of homeless persons during the 1980's and 1990's, in general, and families with children in particular. These include: Diminishing numbers of low income housing units, a reduction in social welfare and education programs, deinstitutionalization of the mentally ill, and changes in the labor market.

It is estimated that 2.5 million people in the United States are homeless with approximately 30% to 50% of this group comprised of families with children (Rosenberg, Solarz, & Bailey, 1991). A disproportionate number of homeless people are minorities and a majority of the homeless families are headed by single mothers (McChesney, 1992).

Although it is difficult to accurately assess the number of homeless school-aged children, the National Coalition for the Homeless (1990) estimates that there are between 500,000-750,000 students. A further breakdown of these statistics show that 54% of homeless youngsters are in grades 7-12 and 45% are in elementary school . Approximately 43% do not attend school on a regular basis (Solarz, 1992).

Homelessness impacts families in many ways. The following case vignette describes some of the common concerns which emerge in families as they try to cope with numerous stressors related to being homeless. This case is compiled from several interviews which were conducted with a group of homeless women and their children residing in the Western region of the United States.

The school counselor at Kaiser Middle School is concerned about a seventh grade student named Candi because she has been absent for most of the quarter. The counselor has tried to contact her parents to set up a conference, but has not been able to get an answer to her repeated phone calls.

When Candi finally shows up at school the counselor informs her that she may not be able to meet the credit requirements to be promoted into the eighth grade. Although she is embarrassed, Candi finally informs the school counselor that her family is living in a tent at a local park. The counselor decides to visit her parents.

Upon reaching the park, she sees a woman in her early thirties with two elementary school-aged children by her side. She has a full length cast on her right leg and is busy yelling instructions to her children. The counselor introduces herself and Candi's mother begins to tell her story. "I have been living in this park for about eight months and it has been really hard on me and the kids. You never know who is going to bother you or try to steal your stuff. There is no privacy here and it is not safe for the children to go into the bathrooms by themselves. Since I fell down it has been hard for me to move around. Luckily I have Candi to help me with the two younger ones and to do the daily chores. My husband left us years ago and so we are on our own."

"I know Candi would rather be in school with her friends, even though some of them give her a hard time about living in the park. Life is stressful for all of us. The money usually does not last the whole month and sometimes we don't even have enough to buy food. I know that you want Candi in school, but who else is going to help me?"

Given their own set of developmental challenges and life stressors, homeless persons are considered to represent a special population of persons. This diverse population group has unique characteristics which define who they are and the types of special needs they have as a result of their homeless status. What follows is a brief discussion of some of the salient features of this group which leads to their classification as a unique diverse population group.

## Homelessness Defined

A person is defined as being homeless if they meet any of the following criteria: they are unable to secure regular and stable housing, their primary place of residence is in a public or private shelter (which is designed to provide "temporary" shelter), or they live in a place that is not ordinarily used for housing such as a car or an abandoned building (National Coalition for the Homeless, 1990). Although homeless people suffer from not having adequate shelter they typically experience a constellation of other problems which help define them as a heterogenous group. Some of these problems and stressors are listed below.

## Common Characteristics and Stressors

In addition to not being able to access affordable housing, homeless people in the United States are plagued by a host of other issues including: poverty, high unemployment rates and low job skills, limited social support networks, and a myriad of social adjustment problems (including substance abuse, domestic violence, and other mental health problems). These economic and social dynamics contribute to a variety of concerns such as poor nutrition and a shortage of food, physical and health problems, issues related to a low level of self-esteem and self-confidence, safety concerns, a lack of privacy, stressful and unpredictable living conditions, and ridicule and social isolation from others (Morse, 1992).

## Research and Counseling Implications

Although the plight of homeless families has been gaining increasing attention over the past decade, research involving persons in this vulnerable population has been very limited within the counseling profession (Daniels, 1995). The transient and heterogeneous nature of homeless people makes it difficult to conduct research on this population. Thus, basic information regarding the exact numbers of homeless persons in various communities, their specific psychological needs, and the types of counseling services that will effectively address their needs is often difficult to accurately assess (Daniels, 1995).

Counselors often feel unprepared to provide comprehensive services to homeless families and their children because of the limited attention this group has received in the counseling literature (Daniels, 1995). In order to learn more about this vulnerable population Daniels (1995) conducted research among homeless families and their children in Hawai'i. The results of this investigation provided counselors with specific guidelines to keep in mind when working with this at-risk group of people. What follows is a list of recommendations for counselors:

1. Assess how the temporary living situation is affecting all of the homeless family members. The specific issues that need to be explored include: Safety concerns, stress associated with transience or substandard living conditions, privacy, and positive outcomes (i.e., being around peers, living in a park setting).
2. Link homeless families with community resources and agencies which have services that address their particular needs (housing, health, food, schooling, day care).
3. Examine specific issues related to health, hygiene, and nutrition. Provide healthy snacks during counseling sessions and help homeless individuals access shower facilities and grooming supplies.
4. When working with homeless children, assess the potential types of stress and conflicts these youth are likely to experience with their peers (i.e., teasing) and parents (i.e., fighting). Provide stress management and conflict resolution training.
5. Use group counseling to help build support networks with other individuals who are also homeless.
6. Teach coping skills to homeless youngsters and their parents.
7. Assist parents with conflict management skills and parent effectiveness training,

these are both useful ways of helping parents learn new methods of reducing familial conflict and stress.

Regardless of the types of counseling approaches used, Daniels' (1995) research findings emphasized the need for counselors to be particularly sensitive to the shame, embarrassment, and stigma that homeless people typically experience.

## Conclusion

The rate of homelessness is likely to escalate as we enter the 21st century. Given this reality, counselors will need to be well equipped to address the multifaceted needs of this group. Working with this vulnerable population will inevitably challenge traditional counseling approaches to become more proactive and preventive. To effectively address the needs of homeless families, counselors are encouraged to develop and implement a variety of community outreach and school-based counseling services.

## References

Daniels, J. (1995). Humanistic interventions for homeless students: Identifying and reducing barriers to their personal development. *The Journal of Humanistic Education and Development*, 33, 164-172.

McChesney, K.Y. (1992). Homeless families: Four patterns of poverty. In M.J. Robertson & M. Greenblatt (Eds.), *Homelessness: A national perspective* (pp. 3-18). New York: Plenum.

Morse, G.A. (1992). Causes of homelessness. In M.J. Robertson & M. Greenblatt (Eds.), *Homelessness: A national perspective* (pp. 3-18). New York: Plenum.

National Coalition for the Homeless (1990). *Homelessness in America: A summary.* Washington, DC: Author.

Rosenberg, A.A., Solarz, A.L., & Bailey, W.A. (1991). Psychology and homelessness: A public policy and advocacy agenda. *American Psychologist*, 46 1239-1244.

Solarz, A.L. (1992). To be young and homeless: Implications of homelessness for children. In M.J. Robertson & M. Greenblatt (Eds.), *Homelessness: A national perspective* (pp. 275-286). New York: Plenum.

# Culture and Diversity in the Netherlands

*Nathan Deen*

## Overview

Prior to 1940, some ethnic diversity had always existed in the Netherlands. However, only since 1945 has immigration had a visible impact on the composition of the population. The position of the Netherlands as a small, largely industrialized country and a major gateway to Europe, has contributed to a continuing pattern of immigration.

The three most important streams of immigration are caused by:
1. decolonization,
2. migrant labor, and
3. the creation of refugees of war and persecution elsewhere.

## Ethnographic Perspectives of the Netherlands

Since the conclusion of Holland's Golden Age (around 1700) with its immigration of many Sephardic Jews and French Huguenots, and until the end of World War II, the population in the Netherlands was fairly homogeneous, consisting of white Europeans. Half of the population was Protestant and the other half Roman Catholic, totaling at the start of World War II some 11 million people. One hundred fifty thousand Jews completed the picture. Of this last group 120,000 became victims of the holocaust.

This picture has changed significantly since 1945. The three streams of immigration named above had a profound impact on the ethnic composition.

## Decolonization

Although it is a small country, the Netherlands has had large colonies in Asia as well as in the Caribbean. Indonesia (at that time the Dutch East-Indies) had a liberation movement that succesfully acquired independence in 1948, although the Dutch government only reluctantly gave way to the pressure. As a result, many who used to work for the colonial regime moved to the Dutch mainland. A special group among them were the Moluccans. Unlike most Indonesians, they adhered to the Christian faith and many served as soldiers in the Dutch Indian army. Through a legal suit against the Dutch government they acquired the right to move to the Netherlands, but refused to accept Dutch citizenship. Instead they established a "Republic of the South Moluccans in exile" (Bartels, 1989).

A second important group came from the Caribbean, especially from Surinam (former Dutch Guyana). During the years immediately preceding Surinam's independence (1975), almost 350,000 Surinamese moved to the Netherlands. This group consists mainly of Blacks of African descent, Indians, and a smaller group of Javanese; this composition reflects the pattern in which the Dutch ruled their Caribbean colonies. Smaller groups have come from the Antilles, which is still part of the Dutch Kingdom. This is a steadily growing group.

## Migrant Labor

After World War II the Dutch economy had to be rebuilt, and under the Marshall plan Dutch society changed from an agricultural to an industrial base. Newly established industries created an immediate need for unskilled or semi-skilled labor which could not be provided by indigenous workers. The problem was solved by recruiting laborers who were unemployed in their own countries, and who hoped to find a financial paradise in Western Europe. Recruiting took place in several rounds. At first, workers were invited from Southern Europe: Italy, the former Yugoslavia, Greece, Spain, and Portugal. The second round crossed the Mediterranean and workers from Morocco and Turkey were recruited. By now, the

Turks have become, by far, the largest group of immigrants, followed by the Surinamese and the Moroccans. To complete the picture, smaller groups such as Cape Verdians and Ghanese have found work in Holland. A sizeable group of Chinese run small businesses like Chinese-Indonesian restaurants, of which there are a large number in the country.

### Refugees

The most recent wave of immigration consists of refugees. Although a small stream of refugees has always entered the country, unrest in Africa and changes in Eastern Europe are the main reasons for the large number of people who now seek asylum in the Netherlands. This has come at a time when the Netherlands has met its need for workers. Furthermore, those who came earlier have been joined by their families. As a result, the government has introduced stricter border policies and scrutinizes thoroughly applications for asylum. The tendency now is to accept only those who seek asylum for political reasons or because of persecution, and to refuse those who are considered primarily as "economic refugees." The immigration of refugees adds considerably to the diversity of nationalities, cultural traditions, and languages spoken in the country. Many of these refugees have been traumatized by losses of beloved family members and have personally experienced persecution (Van der Veer, 1992). In this respect they are different from the groups mentioned earlier. They are also different in that many of them are well-educated middle class people, whereas many of the migrant workers were unskilled and, in some cases, illiterate.

### Demographic and Status Perspectives

Immigrants tend to cluster in the four largest cities and in other industrial areas. Because the immigration patterns described above began over 40 years ago, second and third generation residents of Mediterranean, Indonesian or Caribbean backgrounds are more numerous than the first generation of parents or grandparents, who brought their families here. As a result, language problems have become less dominant than before, because most of the members of the second and third generation are now bilingual. Their status as a group is still low. Although some social and economic climbing is evident, the education system has not succeeded in providing the children of the migrants educational achievement comparable with the achievement of indigenous children. This may be due partly to home environments that are not conducive to learning. However, these children's overrepresentation in special education makes one suspicious that many probably are underachievers, and that the system does not care for them properly.

The social progress is uneven. The Caribbean and Indonesian immigrants integrate best, which is understandable because they were already familiar with Dutch language and culture before they came to Holland. Usually their educational performance is comparable with the mainstream. Sometimes, they experience racism because of their obvious difference in skin color. The second and third generations from Southern Europe have also become part of society; only their names show Italian or Greek or Spanish background. With all these groups, many ethnic intermarriages have taken place. The situation of those of Turkish and Moroccan descent is different. One reason may be that they have been raised in an environment that tries to stick to tradition. Another reason could be that most of these parents came from agricultural backcountry, producing in this generation severe estrangement as they found themselves in a Western urban area instead of a rural Islamic village. On the whole, Turkish youth perform better in school than do Moroccan, for unclear reasons.

Rising unemployment rates in the Netherlands (currently approximately 11%) sometimes ignites hostile feelings toward minority groups who serve as convenient scapegoats for the problems associated with unemployment and the scarcity of housing.

### Government Policies

In the first decades that migrant workers were introduced in the country, this was seen by the government as temporary. It was expected that most workers would return to their home country and live happy ever after. It did not work that way. After some time, the government was pressured to reunite families, and allow spouses and children to join the workers. Only since the 1980's have government policies recognized that these immigrants are here to stay. At first, schools focussed on teaching Dutch as a second language, and provided for teaching of background language and culture. Career guidance tended to stimulate pupils to choose schools and trades that would be useful upon returning to their parents' country of origin. Recently, the focus has shifted to policies that help past and recent immigrants and their children to become familiar with the Dutch society and to acquire full citizenship. Immigrants have gained voting rights in their communities, while a slowly growing number has applied for Dutch nationality. (The Caribbean immigrants always had Dutch nationality.)

The government also made available funds to develop special provisions for immigrant children in the schools; oftentimes these funds are supplemented by local governments. This way, special programs could be developed to help children in finding their way through the school curriculum and to realize more of their potential, thereby upgrading their performance in and out of school settings.

### Guidance and Counseling

Life is complicated for ethnic minority children in Dutch schools. The same is true for their teachers and counselors. The diversity in some classrooms and schools is immense, 15-20 different languages spoken and culturally operating in a single classroom is not unusual. Teachers need to learn how to handle this, and how to understand cultural differences. Hofstede's dimensions (Hofstede, 1991) may be used as a training device to help teachers find their way. The relationship with ethnic minority parents is not always easily developed, especially if the teacher is female. Sometimes the home environment is very strict, and the school will be considered too permissive.The mix of boys and girls may raise problems with the parents, as may the sports outfits used for physical education.

Some practical rules that apply here are the following:

1. Develop awareness of your own biases toward the culturally different.
2. Develop an awareness of the culturally different dimensions of cultures you work with in comparison with your own.
3. Be aware that an individual person should never be treated on the basis of cultural stereotypes.
4. In case of conflicting values respect those that do not contradict human rights.

Some teacher and counselor education programs now offer course modules to introduce teachers and teacher-trainees into these areas. In some cities schools have "ethnic liaison officers" whose job it is to link home and school and assist parents, pupils, and teachers to find their way in the complex realm of education. Proposals are currently underway that have the support of teachers' unions to extend this kind of provisions to more schools.

### Conclusion

The successful inclusion of cultural diversity in Dutch education and counseling policies and programs presents the Netherlands with a challenge as well as an opportunity. The situation remains complex and will offer us an opportunity to develop our society (including its education and counseling policies and programs) in ways that enable all cultural groups, including the Dutch, to live together in a humane and respectful way, while contributing aspects of their respective heritages to the wellbeing of the entire society.

### Note

For obvious reasons, most literature on this subject is written in the Dutch language. I have tried to put in references to literature written in English that will be accessible to the readers of this chapter. I apologize for the fact that not everything mentioned in this chapter can be adequately referenced for this reason.

## References

Berg-Eldering, L. van den, F. J. M. de Rijcke, & L. V. Zuck (Eds.). (1983). *Multicultural education: A challenge for teachers.* Dordrecht, Netherlands: Foris Publications.

Bartels, D. (1989). *Moluccans in exile: A struggle for ethnic survival.* Leiden, Netherlands: C.O.M.T.

Cross, M. (1994). *Ethnic pluralism and racial inequality: A comparison of colonial and industrial societies.* Utrecht, Netherlands: ISOR.

Frankrijker, H. de, & Frankrijer, F. K. (1992). *Education in a multicultural society.* De Lier, Netherlands: Academic Book Center.

Hofstede, G. (1991). *Cultures and organizations: Software of the mind.* Maidenhead, UK: McGraw Hill.

Muus, P. J. (1994). *Immigrants and policies in the Netherlands: Recent trends and developments.* Amsterdam, Netherlands: Centre for Migration Research UVA.

Van der Veer, G. (1992). *Counselling and therapy with refugees.* Chichester, UK: John Wiley.

# Lesbian, Gay, and Bisexual Identity Issues

*Christine Browning*

## Overview

There has been a tremendous change in how the mental health profession has addressed lesbian, gay, bisexual issues in the past 25 years. In the early 1970's, the American Psychiatric Association removed homosexuality from the *Diagnostic and Statistical Manual of Psychiatric Disorders* as a mental disorder. Since then numerous policy statements by the mental health professional associations have been written to depathologize lesbian, gay, and bisexual identity. These policies have been useful in challenging myths and stereotypes, which continue to be associated with homosexuality. Research efforts have also shifted from examining etiology or conversion to gaining information about the richness and complexity of lesbian, gay, and bisexual lives.

## Unique Features of Lesbian, Gay, and Bisexual Identity

People with a lesbian, gay, or bisexual identity are not generally born into a family or community with others who share the same identity. Consequently, transmission of values, norms, and coping strategies needed to live as a sexual minority in a heterosexual culture is not typically available. Furthermore, disclosure of one's sexual orientation identity sometimes results in the loss of family and community (Brown, 1989).

Unlike an ascribed identity (which is recognized or acknowledged from birth) a gay, lesbian, or bisexual identity is discovered or achieved during the lifespan (Weinberg & Williams, 1974). Since a lesbian, gay or bisexual identity is generally invisible it requires overt disclosure to others for recognition. There are stressors associated with having an invisible identity such as deciding when and how to reveal to others and being exposed to homo-negative comments or threats.

## Demographics

Precise estimates of the percentages of people with a lesbian, gay, and bisexual identity aredifficult to report because of problems with sampling methodology. Gonsiorek & Weinrich (1991) report estimates that from 4% to 17% of all men and women in the United States are homosexual. Although there are many stereotypes associated with a gay, lesbian or bisexual identity, in reality there is tremendous diversity of experiences among lesbian, gay, and bisexual people (eg. age, race/ethnicity, gender, class, physical ability, religious and political beliefs, education, geographic location, and other personal characteristics and life experiences).

The tenacity of the stereotypes is often aided by the lack of gay visibility to counter the perceptions. This invisibility occurs because of the fears and experiences of societal discrimination and homo-hatred targeted toward lesbian, gay, and bisexual people. In addition, major societal institutions (i.e., legal, religious, family, media, education, medical) at best render invisible the lives of lesbian, gay, and bisexual people. At worst these institutions denigrate gay lives and attempt to make their existence illegal or immoral.

## Coming-Out Process

Gay, lesbian, or bisexual people are socialized in the dominant heterosexual culture and are expected to adopt heterosexual norms and goals for adult development. Expectations for heterosexual dating, courtship, marriage, and procreation are also intrinsically linked to cultural expectations for gender role conformity. Deviation from heterosexual expectations or strict adherence of gender role behavior can result in family or societal disapproval, rejection, harassment or actual acts of physical violence. Lack of federal and state laws to ensure basic civil rights for lesbian, gay, and bisexual people often serve to reinforce institutional discrimination (Herek, 1989).

At the same time that lesbian, gay or bisexual people are dealing with heterosexual and cultural expectations, they may experience a growing awareness of same gender interest or attraction. For some, this awareness becomes apparent in early childhood while others may not become aware of their feelings until adolescence or adulthood (Garnets & Kimmel, 1991). Consequently, the coming out process (self identification of a lesbian, gay, or bisexual identity and disclosure to family, friends, co-workers, and others) will be experienced differently based upon the individual's characteristics. The developmental tasks of the coming out process identified by many theorists and summarized by Garnets & Kimmel (1991) include transforming a societally stigmatized identity into a positive identity; exploration and socialization in the gay community; disclosure to others; managing one's identity in a heterosexist environment; and building a family and community for support.

Although there are some common developmental tasks associated with the coming out process, the experience will vary depending upon individual variables, concurrent developmental tasks of adulthood, and ethnic and gender identity development (Browning, 1987). The following three case examples will illustrate how coming out may be experienced differently as a function of contextual factors:

1. a 14-year old African American youth living in a rural, Southern farming community with his Christian fundamentalist family;
2. a 25-year old Jewish, Caucasian, deaf woman who is a graduate student in a progressive college in a large metropolitan area; and
3. a 45-year old third generation, Japanese American woman married, with children living in a middle class suburban neighborhood who finds herself in love with her best woman friend, while still in love with her husband.

Each of these people would face different challenges at arriving at a positive lesbian, gay or bisexual identity depending upon the availability of community support, access to information, personal and cultural beliefs about homosexuality or bisexuality, and reactions by their family, friends, and communities. The notion that there is one singular lesbian, gay, or bisexual "lifestyle" is erroneous. There is a richness of individual lesbian, gay, and bisexual experiences and some unifying experiences based on the experience of having a minority group identity.

**Counseling Implications**

The American Psychological Association Task Force on Heterosexual Bias in Psychotherapy documented practices by psychotherapists that reflected biased, inappropriate, or inadequate treatment toward lesbian and gay clients. The report also provided examples of gay affirmative practice (Garnets, Hancock, Cochran, Goodchilds, & Peplau, 1991). As a result, the Task Force has begun to develop guidelines for practice with lesbian, gay, and bisexual clients to help clinicians provide competent, ethical services.

The following is a list derived from several authors (Browning, Reynolds, Dworkin, 1991; Falco, 1991; Walsh, 1995) who have provided suggestions about working with lesbian, gay, and bisexual clients:

1. examine one's own biases and values about sexual orientation;
2. learn about the coming out process and available community resources;
3. explore how the client's sexual orientation is related or unrelated to the presenting concern;
4. understand the client's sexual orientation identity within the context of relevant religious and cultural values, gender

socialization and other adult developmental tasks;

5. utilize support and other specialized groups by ethnicity, age, specific clinical topics (i.e., 12-step programs, grief, coming out groups) to break down isolation and alienation;

6. use bibliotherapy and facilitate contact with others who may serve as role models for successful identity integration;

7. assist clients in overcoming shameful feelings about their identity by increasing their understanding about internalized homophobia and the interconnections between other forms of oppression;

8. encourage clients to develop ties with a larger community that supports their identity;

9. help clients develop skills to cope with anti-gay discrimination in society; and

10. help clients to develop dating and relationship skills.

## Training

Although it has been over 20 years since the mental health professions have considered homosexuality or bisexuality as evidence of pathology, the systematic training of mental health practitioners about lesbian, gay, and bisexual issues has been minimal. Few graduate programs offer course work or supervision and research opportunities in lesbian, gay, and bisexual issues (Buhrke & Douce, 1991).

There has been a proliferation of psychological information developed over the past 20 years that can help mental health professionals learn to 1) identify the unique stressors and strengths of people with a lesbian, gay, or bisexual identity, and 2) develop the necessary skills to provide sensitive and competent therapeutic interventions. In addition, mental health professionals are encouraged by the major professional organizations to assume advocacy roles by using our professional knowledge to help change negative societal attitudes that serve as

foundations for discrimination and harassing behavior toward lesbian, gay, and bisexual people.

## Conclusion

Lesbian, gay and bisexual people reflect all aspects of human diversity (i.e., age, race/ethnicity, class, education, physical ability status, religion, geographic location). There are unique stressors related to the experience of being gay, lesbian or bisexual and living in a predominately heterosexual culture that provides rewards for heterosexual identity.

The various coming out models provide some guidance in identifying common tasks and challenges inherent in developing a positive lesbian, gay, or bisexual identity. It is important however, to contextualize the coming out process by considering other individual variables and adult developmental tasks.

## References

Brown, L. S. (1989). Lesbians, gay men and their families: Common clinical issues. *Journal of Gay and Lesbian Psychotherapy, 1*, 65-78.

Browning, C., Reynolds, A., Dworkin, S. (1991). Affirmative psychotherapy for lesbian women. *The Counseling Psychologist, 19* (2), 177-196.

Browning, C. (1987). Therapeutic issues and intervention strategies with young adult lesbian clients: A developmental approach. *Journal of Homosexuality, 14*, 45-52.

Buhrke, R. & Douce, L. (1991). Training issues for counseling psychologists in working with lesbian women and gay men. *The Counseling Psychologist, 19*, 216-234.

Falco, K. (1991). *Psychotherapy with lesbian clients: Theory into practice.* NY: Brunner/Mazel.

Garnets, L., Hancock, K. A., Cochran, S., Goodchilds, J., & Peplau, L. A. (1991). Issues in psychotherapy with lesbians and gay men. *American Psychologist, 46*, 964-972.

Garnets, L. D. & Kimmel, D. C. (1991). Lesbian and gay male dimensions in the psychological study of human diversity. In J.D. Goodchilds (Ed.), *Psychological perspectives on human diversity in America* (pp. 143-192). Washington, DC: American Psychological Association.

Gonsiorek, J. & Weinrich, J. (1991). The definition and scope of sexual orientation. In J. Gonsiorek, & J. Weinrich, (Eds.), *Homosexuality: Research implications for public policy* (pp. 1-12). Newbury Park, CA: Sage.

Herek, G. (1989). Hate crimes against lesbians and gay men: Issues for research and policy. *American Psychologist, 44,* 948-955.

Walsh, P. (1995) *Biased and affirmative practice with lesbian and gay clients.* Unpublished Master's thesis, California State University, Long Beach.

Weinberg, M.S. & Williams, C. (1974). *Male homosexuals: Their problems and adaptations.* NY: Oxford University Press.

# Refugee Mental Health and Psychotherapy

*Fred Bemak*

### Overview

The migration of refugees is a difficult and frequently turbulent process. Many refugees from Africa, Asia, the Caribbean, Eastern Europe, and Latin America have relocated in an attempt to flee from political persecution, repression, and intolerable situations. As a result of this forced migration, some refugees have exhibited serious mental health problems caused by critical, life-threatening events in their countries of origin. Difficulties in adjusting to dramatically different cultures, changes in family structure, shifts in traditional gender roles, changes in socioeconomic status and employment, language barriers, and overall difficulties in understanding and mastering the daily life in a new and strange environment have further exacerbated psychological problems (Chung & Kagawa-Singer, 1993; Lin, Masuda, & Tazuma, 1982). A combination of mandatory acculturation, refugee status, forced migration, and associated trauma have given refugees a unique cultural identity.

In comparison to the general population, refugees have a higher incidence of psychopathology, depression, posttraumatic stress disorder, anxiety, and other psychological problems (Kinzie, 1993; Weisaeth & Eitinger, 1993). Despite their higher rates of mental health problems, many refugees are unwilling to seek help from mainstream psychotherapists and counselors (Chung & Lin, 1994). The first choice of treatment for more serious personal or family problems, after consultations with family members, elders, and social support networks, usually begins with explorations of traditional cultural healing methods, that is, religious and/or traditional healers. It is usually after unsuccessful attempts with traditional healing that contact is made with mainstream mental health services.

Western mental health services may present their own set of problems. There may be formidable difficulties in accessing clinics and offices (Chung & Lin, 1994). Once reaching a psychotherapist's office the refugee may experience culturally insensitive staff who are unaware of the effects of their interactions with refugees, such as inappropriate eye contact, speaking too loudly, initiating handshakes, physical touching, managing language barriers, or misinterpreting nonverbal behavior. More specifically, professional counselors may not be cognizant of important customs which may be insulting to the refugee client such as putting one's hand on the shoulder of a woman of Islamic faith or touching the head of a child who was raised in the Buddhist faith in Asia. When the mental health professional requires a translator for psychotherapy, the roles must be carefully defined in order to establish a well balanced and structured partnership to help the client. Therefore, the psychotherapist must not only have therapeutic skills, but must also be knowledgeable and aware of the cultural history, contemporary problems, and realities which the refugee faces in the adjustment process.

### Culture and Mental Health

To provide mental health services for refugees, understanding cultural context is essential. Clinical interventions must be consistent with the fundamental cultural beliefs and values of the refugee's country of origin. Kleinman & Good (1985) have emphasized the need to understand, accept, and confirm the client's cultural conceptualization of their problem. Pedersen (1988) has elaborated on the need to develop and implement culturally sensitive interventions and skills.

### Acculturation and Psychosocial Adjustment

Acculturation generally takes into account stress, adaptation, social indicators, and various models which have been developed, including assimilation, biculturalism, rejection, and deculturation. The general consensus among researchers is that bicultural models of adaptation have been the most effective in generating healthy psychological outcomes for refugees (Berry, 1986; Szapocznik & Kurtines, 1980). Premigration trauma is a significant factor affecting refugee mental health and adjustment. Mollica, Wyshak, & Lavelle (1987) outlined four categories of trauma which are associated with psychological problems and post-migration trauma. This final phase in the migration process may produce culture shock accompanied by feelings of helplessness and confusion. Furthermore, the change from an individualistic to a collectivistic culture (Triandis, 1990) may present difficulties as refugees shift their reference groups (Bemak & Greenberg, 1994).

Other problems may intensify complications with adjustment such as survivor's guilt, difficulties in understanding and learning a new language, lack of applicable skills or professional training, and professional qualifications which are not transferable to the country of resettlement (Chung & Okazaki, 1991). Additional challenges faced by refugee families include the following: children may acculturate faster than their parents due to greater cultural exposure through school and peers, causing shifts in family dynamics as the younger members act as the "cultural bridge" for the family; women sometimes adopt values of the predominant culture which may encourage greater independence and subsequent serious disruptions in traditional family roles; parents and children may argue about conflicting cultural values such as curfews, dating, or marriage; and based on past trauma, refugee children may have difficulties with peers (Ajdukovic & Ajdukovic,

1993; Boothby, 1994; Dadfar, 1994).

It is within the context of coming to terms with pre and post-migration experiences that psychosocial adjustment takes place. The first 1-2 years of resettlement has been recognized as a crucial time in the adjustment process (Tayabas & Pok, 1983). During this time, refugees must unlearn previous adaptive behaviors which may appear pathological or antisocial in the new society (Stein, 1986). Bemak (1989) outlined a three-phase model of acculturation affecting psychosocial adjustment which establishes emotional safety and security through initial cultural skill development, integration of previously learned skills from the country of origin and new skills from the resettlement country, and, finally, creating skills and values that foster a realistic acquisition of future goals.

### Clinical Implications: Model of Psychotherapy

Effective psychotherapy for the refugee entails a clear understanding of individual and family culture, premigration history and experience, and the interrelationship refugees have with their culture. Such understanding not only requires a foundation of knowledge in counseling and psychotherapy, but also dictates a multidisciplinary approach which incorporates constructs in anthropology, psychiatry, public health, social work, and sociology. Furthermore, it is necessary to understand Posttraumatic Stress Disorders and the field of Multicultural Counseling. In order to incorporate these diverse bases of knowledge and skills, Bemak, Chung, and Bornemann (in press) have designed a comprehensive approach to counseling refugees called the Multi-Level Model (MLM). The MLM includes the following four phases: Level I: Mental Health Education; Level II: Individual, Group, and/or Family Psychotherapy; Level III: Cultural Empowerment; and Level IV: Indigenous Healing. There is no fixed sequence to implementing the four levels and they may be used simultaneously or independently. It is important to note that the usage of this model does not require additional funding or resources, but rather it is anticipated that the psychotherapist assumes a more diverse role as a helper.

In Level I, the psychotherapist educates the client(s) about the practice of mental health. Since many refugees are not aware of the process of mental health interventions, this helps them to understand the therapeutic relationship and to formulate expectations for counseling. Level II originated in traditional Western individual, group, and family mental health therapy. It is based upon Western practices of conventional psychotherapy. Drawing on the clinical assessment and the cultural background of the client, the therapist would determine which type(s) of therapy, that is, individual, group, or family, would be most beneficial for the client. Regardless of the choice of therapy, some specific techniques have been found to be helpful for refugees, such as cognitive-behavioral interventions, storytelling, projective drawing, picture interpretations, dreamwork, role playing, relaxation, more active direct interventions, gestalt, and psychodrama. Level III provides another important dimension in the healing of the refugee — cultural empowerment. Frequently the therapist will focus on mental health concerns while neglecting basic issues of adaptation to daily life. Cultural empowerment directly addresses these adjustment problems by requiring the counselor to assume the role of a "cultural guide," by translating information, and by answering questions about the new environment. Level IV, indigenous healing, is when the psychotherapist integrates Western and traditional healing methodologies, according to the nature of the problem and cultural background of the refugee. This is done in cooperation with indigenous healers who are known to refugee community members, thus fostering an expansion beyond the customary western practices of psychotherapy. (Case examples are given in Bemak, Chung, Pedersen and Bornemann, in press).

## Conclusion

Psychotherapy with refugees presents the mental health professional with complex challenges. The history and experience of the refugee is unique, requiring extensive knowledge about cross-cultural psychotherapy, posttraumatic stress, and different societies. Understanding the background of the refugee experience is crucial to effective psychotherapy. The Multi-Level Model (MLM) provides a framework which integrates psychoeducational training, adjustment through cultural empowerment, and indigenous healing methods with Western individual, group, and family psychotherapy, taking into account the diverse and complicated psychological needs of the refugee.

## References

Ajdukovic M., & Ajdukovic, D. (1993). Psychological well-being of refugee children. *Child Abuse and Neglect, 17*, 843-854.

Bemak, F. (1989). Cross-cultural family therapy with Southeast Asian refugees. *Journal of Strategic and Systemic Therapies, (8)*, 22-27.

Bemak, F., Chung, R.C-Y., & Bornemann, T. (in press). Counseling and psychotherapy with refugees. In P. Pedersen, J. Draguns, W. Lonner, & J. Trimble (Eds.), *Counseling Across Cultures* (4th ed.). Thousand Oaks, CA: Sage Publications.

Bemak, F., Chung, R. C-Y., Pedersen, P., & Bornemann, T. (in press). *Multicultural counseling of refugees: A case study approach to innovative interventions.* Thousands Oaks, CA: Sage Publications.

Bemak, F. & Greenberg, B. (1994). Southeast Asian refugee adolescents: Implications for counseling. *Journal of Multicultural Counseling and Development, 22* (4), 115-124.

Berry, J. W. (1986). The acculturation process and refugee behavior. In C. L. Williams & J. Westermeyer (Eds.), *Refugee mental health in resettlement countries* (pp. 25-37). Washington, DC: Hemisphere.

Boothby, N. (1994). Trauma and violence among refugee children. In A. J. Marsella, T. Bornemann, S. Ekblad, & J. Orley (Eds.), *Amidst peril and pain: The mental health and well-being of the world's refugees* (pp. 239-259). Washington, DC: American Psychological Association.

Chung, R. C-Y., & Kagawa-Singer, M. (1993). Predictors of psychological distress among Southeast Asian refugees. *Social Science and Medicine, 36*(5), 631-639.

Chung, R. C-Y., & Lin, K. M. (1994). Helpseeking behavior among Southeast Asian refugees. *Journal of Community Psychology, 22,* 109-120.

Chung, R. C-Y., & Okazaki, S. (1991). Counseling Americans of Southeast Asian descent: The impact of the refugee experience. In C. C. Lee & B. L. Richardson (Eds.), *Multicultural issues in counseling: New approaches to diversity* (pp.107-126). Alexandria, VA: American Association for Counseling and Development.

Dadfar, A. (1994). The Afghans: Bearing the scars of a forgotten war. In A. J. Marsella, T. Bornemann, S. Ekblad, & J. Orley (Eds.), *Amidst peril and pain: The mental health and well-being of the world's refugees* (pp. 125-139). Washington, DC: American Psychological Association.

Kinzie, D. (1993). Posttraumatic effects and their treatment among Southeast Asian refugees. In J. Wilson & B. Raphael (Eds.), *International handbook of traumatic stress syndromes* (pp. 311-320). New York: Plenum Press.

Kleinman, A. & Good, B. (1985). *Culture and depression: Studies in the anthropology and cross-cultural psychiatry of affect and disorder.* Berkeley: University of California Press.

Mollica, R. F., Wyshak, G. & Lavelle, J. (1987). The psychosocial impact of war trauma and torture on Southeast Asian refugees. *American Journal of Psychiatry, 144* (12), 1567-1572.

Pedersen, P. (1988). *A handbook for developing multicultural awareness.* Alexandria, VA: American Association for Counseling and Development.

Stein, B. N. (1986). The experience of being a refugee: Insights from the research literature. In C. L. Williams & J. Westermeyer (Eds.), *Refugee mental health in resettlement countries* (pp. 5-23). Washington, DC: Hemisphere.

Szapocznik, J. & Kurtines, W. (1980). Acculturation, biculturalism, and adjustment among Cuban-Americans. In A. M. Padilla (Ed.) *Recent advances in acculturation research: Theory, models, and some new findings* (pp. 914-931). Boulder, CO: Westview Press.

Tayabas, T. & Pok, T. (1983). The arrival of the Southeast Asian refugees in America: An Overview. In *Bridging cultures: Southeast Asian refugees in America* (pp. 3-14). Los Angeles: Special Services for Groups-Asian American Community Mental Health Training Center.

Triandis, H. (1990). Cross cultural studies of individualism and collectivism. In J. Berman (Ed.), *Cross-cultural perspectives* (pp.41-134). Lincoln and London: University of Nebraska Press.

Weisaeth, L., & Eitinger, L. (1993). Posttraumatic stress phenomena. Common themes across wars, disasters, and traumatic events. In J. Wilson & B. Raphael (Eds.), *International handbook of traumatic stress syndromes* (pp. 69-78). New York: Plenum Press.

# The Rural Client

*Richard E. Pearson*
*Beverly A. Burnell*

### Overview

The rural context ranges from small fishing communities, areas centered on the timber industry, dairy country, mining regions, locales in which tourism is the major source of employment, communities whose populations are made up almost entirely of retired persons, and districts dominated by truck farming. These communities combine geographic diversity with variations in ethnicity, race, and religion, and differences between those whose rural background goes back for generations and those who have recently relocated to a rural setting. Taken together, it becomes apparent that when we talk of "rural clients" we must examine specifically the characteristics upon which we are focusing. Against the realities of this variety overlaying variety, are there commonalities among rural clients that can serve as useful guides, beyond that offered by the long-honored admonition to "take the internal frame of reference?"

### Counseling-Relevant Perspectives

On the basis of our experience in rural settings, and a familiarity with the relevant literature relating to counseling and human service interventions, we propose the following four issues as important dimensions of the rural experience. These issues cut across geographic and personological variables sufficiently enough to be useful in understanding the outlook and responses of the rural people with whom we work:

1. isolation;
2. the primacy of face-to-face exchange;
3. the importance of place; and
4. a pragmatic view of helping and change.

These interrelated factors can serve as useful reference points to counselors and other helping professionals approaching the task of relating to, and forging productive alliances with, clients who have been shaped by rural life, as well as those who have recently adopted rural living.

### Isolation

The census bureau identifies a rural community as "non-metro," a community not located in a Standard Metropolitan Service Area (SMSA). SMSA's are communities consisting of a central city of 50,000 or more and their surrounding suburbs (DeYoung, 1994). By this definition, rural communities are geographically distant from large cities and their suburbs. They make up 25% of the total U.S. population. Connecting with services and information, which are taken for granted in more populated areas, becomes more challenging in rural areas due to these greater distances. Roads are generally in poor condition and the absence of regular public transportation options and limited television access (the advent of the satellite dish notwithstanding) further compound rural isolation.

One consequence of this relative isolation is that rural people are often faced with enormous barriers to accessing medical and mental health resources. Isolation cuts rural residents off from knowledge of options that may be relevant to dealing with life issues they face. The limited number of occupations and lifestyles represented in a rural community may make it difficult for young people to envision career and lifestyle choices that would match their talents and interests (Rich, 1979). For example, young women struggling with decisions about careers, marriage, and motherhood have few models of women who have found a way to integrate work, family, and community roles in their daily functioning. Many rural people maintain traditional expectations about appropriate occupations and lifestyles from which the young men and women in their communities might choose, resulting in the further limitation of possibilities (Brown, 1985).

### The Primacy of Face-to-Face Exchange

Though they may cover enormous physical areas, rural communities are typically small in terms of the number of people who comprise them. As Barker and Gump (1964) have noted with regard to rural schools, there are usually as many social roles to be filled as in larger, more populated settings, but fewer people to fill those roles. Distance from the top to the bottom of the various social hierarchies that are found in rural communities tends to be smaller, and overlap of membership among those hierarchies (e.g., between the school and the church) is frequent.

The sense of belonging and community that many rural residents report, is a positive consequence of living in a setting where "everyone knows everyone." By extending that phrase to "where everyone knows everyone's business" we highlight a negative aspect of living in a small, relatively non-complex setting in which direct, face-to-face contacts are possible—a lack of privacy and social "space."

The importance of highly personalized and less formal social institutions can affect the counselor in many ways (Elrod, 1994). For example, the impact of "opinion shapers" (be they clergy, town or county officers, or a school board member) in the community may enormously influence how a counselor is viewed and the extent to which people in the community will seek his or her services. Alternatively, a relative lack of anonymity and cover may make it difficult for potential clients to seek counseling, especially if such assistance is viewed as a sign of weakness or failure in the community.

The rural counselor (whether working in a school or a community clinic) is apt to encounter clients within a wide range of social settings, ranging from recreation to banking. We have frequently had counselors tell us that this inability to get away from their work is a major reason for not living in the rural community in which they practice. This preference of counselors who are rural transplants may conflict with the needs and preferences of indigenous rural community members to "know" and include the counselors in the life of the community beyond their professional interactions (McIntire, Marion, & Quaglia, 1990).

### The Importance of Place

Certainly, rural living is not always an ongoing bucolic holiday as many transplanted "outsiders" can attest. However, we often find rural people holding deep emotional attachments to the physical setting in which they live. Perhaps we see this most strongly in the significance of sacred places to Native Americans, and find it as well in the feelings of farm families whose ties to their land go back many generations.

This sense of place or attachment to the land may comprise a major element of rural clients' identity and feelings of significance (Wilson & Peterson, 1988). That centrality can contribute to self-esteem. It can also stand as an important element in decisions about whether or not to act on personal alternatives and move away from the place in which one was raised. The emotional (and sometimes spiritual) toll of moving away from one's home may far outweigh the social and economic benefits of leaving.

### A Pragmatic View of Helping and Change

Rural people, families, and communities tend to be self-reliant, focusing on cooperative and social approaches to problem-solving. Learning, both formal and informal, is a social activity most successfully undertaken with maximum personal contact and minimal individual recognition and competition (Bloodsworth & Fitzgerald, 1993; Brown, 1985). Learning outcomes are expected to be both global and concrete, a style often resulting in persons questioning "Why is this important for me to do?" Inexperience with social complexity can inhibit any client's willingness to take risks.

Reluctance to seek out assistance from mental health specialists is not unique to rural persons; however, the counselor who works with rural persons may find any reluctance heightened by the reality that the very notion of professional assistance for personal difficulties is suspect or is dismissed as irrelevant because past attempts to access such assistance has left potential clients with the belief that another try is not worth the effort. Drawing on the strengths of rural people's preference for cooperative problem-solving approaches can assist a counselor's goal of increasing options for the client, as well as engaging the client's ownership of the process and outcomes (Elrod, 1994).

## Implications for Counseling

Access to the client (and they to us) may be difficult because of physical (e.g., distance) and attitudinal factors (e.g., reluctance to seek outside help). This reality raises the importance of taking services to clients, and of offering services in a context and format that will ameliorate, as much as possible, attitudinal barriers to seeking and receiving counseling assistance.

Mainstream definitions of "progress" that center on change, growth, and efficiency may not be accepted by rural clients as unquestioned good. Challenging local givens and preferences, and demonstrating relevant but unrecognized options, needs to be done in a manner that draws on the strengths of local perspectives. Interventions must demonstrate how actualization of potential and pursuit of change can be consistent with the rural client's strong sense of place and relationships.

Movement to new settings is often difficult when:
1. a rich, but relatively narrow experience results in a lack of relevant knowledge and skill for easing such transitions;
2. it means separation from settings that are important to a sense of self; and
3. it involves separation from family and community.

Pre-transition assistance helps rural clients develop an accurate understanding of the transition and aids them in creating coping strategies (e.g., a new personal support system). Counselors can also proactively work within both the "old" context (e.g., family) and the "new" context (e.g., college or work setting) to prepare clients for the transition issues of rural persons.

## Case Study

Carl is a sophomore who attends a school in a small, single town school district. The nearest urban area is a city of 28,000 located 25 miles away. Group tests show him to have average intelligence and somewhat below average achievement. His high school grades are significantly below what we would expect from his test scores. While he is not a behavior problem in school, his teachers observe that he could do much better work than he does. He says he doesn't see the need to get really good grades since he plans to go to work right after graduation in the same small manufacturing plant where his father, mother, and one uncle are employed doing routine, unskilled assembly work.

From his perspective, and that of his family, Carl doesn't have a problem with regard to career and lifestyle plans. In contrast, several of his teachers believe that Carl has the intellectual resources to do much "better" than settling into a low-skill, low-paying job in a factory that will probably be automated out of existence within a decade. The school counselor identifies Carl as one of many students in the school who, because of his low level of aspiration, is at risk for eventually developing what the counselor has observed to be a locally-prevalent pattern of underemployment, work-adjustment problems, substance abuse, and family dysfunction. When he reported to his parents that his technology teacher voiced the opinion that he had the ability to learn a skilled trade, they told him to tell the teacher to mind his own business.

Carl presents us with many issues; for example, the influence of a tightly-knit family, the paucity of models for alternative behavior, the attractiveness of readily available options, and a lack of openness to change. Perhaps the central problem he presents to the counselor is how the "new" can be introduced in a way that actually allows it to be considered and weighed by him and the people who are important to him, rather than being rejected outright as irrelevant and/or detrimental.

## References

Barker, R. G., & Gump, P. V. (1964). *Big school, small school.* Stanford, CA: Stanford University Press.

Bloodsworth, G., & Fitzgerald, D. (1993). *Preparing teachers for the rural world.* (ERIC Document Reproduction Service No. ED 366 588)

Brown, D. E. (1985). *Higher education students from rural communities: A report on dropping out.* U. S. Department of Education, National Institute of Education. (ERIC Document Reproduction Service No. ED 258 771)

DeYoung, A. J. (1994). Children at risk in America's rural schools: Economic and cultural dimensions. In R. J. Rossi (Ed.), *Schools and students at risk: Context and framework for positive change* (p. 251). New York, NY: Teachers College.

Elrod, G. F. (1994). Infusing rural school-community partnerships into transition components of individualized education plans: Processes and outcomes. (ERIC Document Reproduction Service No. ED 369 620)

McIntire, W. G., Marion, S. F., & Quaglia, R. (1990). Rural school counselors: Their communities and schools. *The School Counselor, 37,* 166-172.

Rich, N. S. (1979). Occupational knowledge: To what extent is rural youth handicapped? *The Vocational Guidance Quarterly, 27,* 320-325.

Wilson, S. M., & Peterson, G. W. (1988). Life satisfaction among young adults from rural families. *Family Relations, 37,* 84-91.

# Social Class as a Basis for Prescriptive Intervention

*Arnold P. Goldstein*

### Overview

The mental health, education, and socialization of adolescents and younger children have been the joint concerns of many professionals, psychologists, teachers, counselors, social workers, and others. A common reflection of such concern has been the attempt to identify increasingly satisfactory means by which each educational, therapeutic, and remedial profession can carry out its helping mission. Although it is indeed both appropriate and highly desirable that helping and educational professions continually seek to improve their effectiveness, careful examination of relevant literature within each of the fields noted above reveals a common and distressing theme—the one-true-light assumption (Goldstein, & Stein, 1976; Kiesler, 1966). This is the recurrent tendency on the part of developers and disciples of given treatment and teaching methods to overextend the applicability of the given method, to claim its usefulness with too many disparate types of clients, and (also in the absence of sufficient supporting evidence) to explicitly or implicitly discourage or disparage the usefulness of other methods.

Thus, at various times, group psychotherapy has been viewed as the treatment for all child-abusing parents; process training has for some writers been the exclusive prescription for all learning disabilities; guided group interaction and positive peer culture have at different times been described as the "one true light" for all juvenile delinquency; play therapy and now various behavior modification techniques have been claimed as the answer for all emotional disturbance; and elementary education has had its periods during which indirect teaching, learning by discovery, and open education have held singular sway.

The singularity of applied orientation and procedural tunnel vision that constitute these examples of the one-true-light assumption seem to have their roots, in part, in the unidimensionality or unimethodology of many clinical and counseling training centers and schools of education. Change agents are all too often taught the real and purported virtues of only a single orientation or cluster of approaches, such teaching being done by trusted, powerful, and rewarded models. Once planted, the one-true-light assumption grows as a function of the change agent needing to see himself or herself, as well as the client, in specified ways.

The change agent's need for a consistent working strategy, for minimal cognitive dissonance in daily functioning, for the familiar, for what appears to be useful in attaining the rewards earned by earlier models, and, on occasion, for omnipotence are all bases for overadherence to a single change orientation. But it is not only practitioner treatment strategy that suffers from such a one-true-light perspective. Kiesler (1966) has called our attention to the patient uniformity myth, which occurs so consistently in the context of adult psychotherapy. This is the tendency on the part of change agents and researchers to blur or ignore interpatient differences and, instead, assume "for purposes of this study" or, "for all practical purposes," an essential similarity between clients who, in fact, are different in ways that are relevant to their treatment dispositions. Analogous uniformity myths appear operative with pupil, delinquent, and child therapy clients. Thus, the one-true-light assumption is essentially a failure of discrimination. The change agent fails to construe either an adequate array of potential change methods or sufficient diversity in the clientele to whom such methods might be applied.

The one-true-light assumption is a costly consequence of indiscriminant analysis. Although there is evidence that a singularity of therapeutic or education orientation is a positive contribution to client change when the given orientation "fits" the client, such singularity is clearly subtractive when it is a "misfit." When the teaching method or counseling technique is discrepant from what is optimal for a given client, when the method or technique is inert or counterproductive, all consequences are negative. At best, time and effort are wasted—time and effort that could have been put to more appropriate prescriptive use. At worst, clients deteriorate needlessly, pupils fall further behind academically, and helpers do little that is positive for their own view of their professional competence. I would, therefore, urge rejection of the one-true-light assumption, both by trainers who promulgate it and change agents who enact it. Instead, I would encourage an operating strategy that seeks to tailor or customize counseling and teaching and that seeks to establish optimal matches of counselors, clients, and counseling methods; of teachers, pupils, and teaching methods; of trainers, trainees, and training methods. I would encourage a strategy that is, in essence, prescriptive.

### Prescriptiveness and Social Class

Being poor in America has serious implications —all negative—for one's housing, nutrition, physical health, and many other core aspects of one's life, including how one is treated at the hands of the nation's mental health establishment. Low-income—as opposed to middle-class—client-applicants seeking mental health services are less likely to be accepted as bona fide clients at, for example, America's almost 800 community mental health centers; are more likely to spend a long period on a waiting list; are more likely to be seen by the agency's least experienced staff members; are more likely to receive a pejoratively toned formal diagnosis; are more likely to hold treatment-relevant expectations at variance with those held by the assigned counselor or therapist; are more likely to form a poor quality relationship with this change agent; and are less likely to

improve as a function of their (usually truncated) counseling participation (Frank, 1961; Goldstein, 1973; Yamamoto & Goin, 1965).

Though the responsibility for such intervention failure is not infrequently placed on the shoulders of the low-income client and his or her purported "resistance," the truth often seems otherwise. A prescriptive mismatch appears to have occurred. The lower-social-class client and his or her typically middle-social-class change agent represent different cultures. Both may be of the same race, ethnicity, age, gender, and city of residence. But if they are from different social classes, they are from different cultures. Further, they are from different cultures in ways that directly bear upon the form and efficacy of the intervention most appropriately offered.

For reasons I will seek to explicate, it is my belief that client and counselor literally see the world of intervention (and beyond) differently, and that such differences in perspective must be factored into intervention selection or development decisions in crucial ways. Following a "many-true-lights orientation" to intervention work will lead to the development of reform prescriptions; that is, an array of prescriptively tailored interventions differentially responsive to relevant client characteristics. Rejected here is a conformity prescription strategy, in which little effort is made to individualize the intervention offered and, instead, attempts are made to socialize or train the client to fit the (unchanged) intervention. Stated otherwise, the preferred strategy urges that we change the therapy to fit the client, not change the client to fit the therapy.

The effort to develop such a reform prescription for low-income clients begins with one's definition of counseling or psychotherapy. Such interventions are, at root, interpersonal, influence-learning experiences. Thus, how clients most effectively learn is a major consideration— in fact, the central consideration—in determining the optimal form of the intervention to be developed. Developmental psychological research amply demonstrates that prototypical socialization practices in socioeconomically middle-class and lower-class U.S. homes differ substantially from one another (Davis, 1967; Hess & Shipman,

1965; Jensen, 1967).As the table below summarizes, the middle-class child is repeatedly taught, both explicitly and implicitly, to look inward and consider the causes or antecedents of his or her behavior (motivation), to look outward and sensitively and accurately decipher the feelings of others with whom he or she is interacting (empathy), and to muster and employ restraint, regulation, and other expressions of self-management (self-control).

*Table*  Social Class and Learning Style

| Middle | Lower | Skillstreaming Procedures |
|--------|-------|---------------------------|
| Motivation | Consequences | Modeling |
| Empathy | Action — — — — | Role Playing |
| Self-Control | External Authority | Performance Feedback |
| | | Transfer Training |

In contrast, it is much more common in the child-rearing characteristic of low-income homes to find a focus on the outcome or results of enacted behaviors (consequences); a direct, concrete, behavioral response to such perceived consequences (action); and a heavy reliance on the urgings, directives, or commands of others, rather than major expectation of self-control (external authority). Thus, the middle-class preadolescent male caught pulling his sister's hair is likely to be asked why he did so (motivation), how he thinks such behavior made his sister feel (empathy), and be reminded that he is old enough to be able to squelch the urge to engage in such behaviors (self-control). The more action-oriented, consequences-oriented, external authority-oriented, low-income parent is apparently substantially more likely to respond to such a perceived transgression by slapping the child—without urging motivational introspection, feeling inspection, or heightened self-control.

What are the counseling and psychotherapy intervention-relevant consequences of these two contrasting child-rearing experiences? Outcome statistics for middle-class clients participating in verbal, insight-oriented psychotherapy or counseling, consistently indicate that approximately two-thirds improve (Bergin &

Lambert, 1978, Luborsky, Singer, & Luborsky, 1975; Meltzoff & Kornreich, 1970; Rachman & Wilson, 1980; Smith & Glass, 1977). I believe that such a felicitous result is at least in substantial part a result of the high degree of correspondence between the learning style (focus on motivation, feelings, self-control, etc.) such clients bring with them to treatment, and the client qualities that are optimal for that treatment to succeed. Low-income clients, with their quite contrasting learning style, do much less well in response to such an intervention approach (Schofield,1964; Yamamoto & Goin, 1965), but might do very well indeed if one followed a reform prescription strategy and offered an intervention tailored to this latter learning style.

This is precisely what I sought to accomplish in 1973 (Goldstein, 1973) with the development of what I then called Structured Learning Therapy, and have since come to call Skillstreaming. Its constituent procedures are modeling, role-playing, performance feedback, and transfer training. As depicted in the preceeding table , each of these procedures prescriptively follows from a major feature of low-income person's characteristic learning style.

In this approach, small groups of youngsters with shared prosocial skill deficiencies are:

1. shown several examples of expert use of the behaviors constituting the skills in which they are weak or lacking (e.g., modeling);
2. given several guided opportunities to practice and rehearse these competent interpersonal behaviors (e.g., role-playing);
3. provided with praise, reinstruction, and related feedback on how well their role-playing of the skill matched the expert model's portrayal of it (e.g., performance feedback); and
4. encouraged to engage in a series of activities designed to increase the chances that skills learned in the training setting will endure and be available for use when needed in the school, home, community, institution or other real-world setting (e.g., transfer training).

113

By means of this set of didactic procedures, it is possible to teach such youngsters a 50-skill curriculum, organized into six groupings:

1. Beginning Social Skills (e.g., "Starting a Conversation," "Introducing Yourself," Giving a Compliment"),
2. Advanced Social Skills (e.g., "Giving Instruction," "Apologizing," "Convincing Others"),
3. Skills for Dealing with Feelings (e.g., "Dealing with Someone Else's Anger," "Expressing Affection," "Dealing with Fear"),
4. Skill Alternative to Aggression (e.g., "Responding to Teasing," "Keeping Out of Fights," "Helping Others"),
5. Skills for Dealing with Stress (e.g., "Dealing with Being Left Out," "Responding to Failure," "Dealing with an Accusation"),
6. Planning Skills (e.g., "Setting a Goal," "Arranging Problems by Importance," "Deciding What Caused a Problem").

My colleagues and I have conducted approximately 30 investigations evaluating the effectiveness of this interpersonal skills training approach. Skill acquisition (Do they learn it?) is a reliable outcome, occurring in well over 90% of the aggressive adolescent and younger child trainees involved (Goldstein, 1981; Goldstein et al., 1980; McGinnis & Goldstein, 1984). Skill transfer (Do they use the skills in real-world setting?) is a less frequent outcome thus far, occurring in about half of the trainees involved. We continue to seek means for increasing the successful generalization of skills-training gains.

### References

Bergin, A. E., & Lambert, M. J. (1978). The evaluation of therapeutic outcomes. In S. L. Garfield & A. E. Bergin (Eds.), *Handbook of psychotherapy and behavior change*. New York: Wiley.

Davis, A. (1967). Language and social class perspectives. In B. Goldstein (Ed.), *Low income youth in urban areas*. New York: Holt.

Frank, J. D. (1961). *Persuasion and healing*. Baltimore: Johns Hopkins Press.

Goldstein, A. P. (1981). *Psychological skill training: The structured learning technique*. Elmsford, NY: Pergamon Press.

Goldstein, A. P. (1973). *Structured learning therapy: Toward a psychotherapy for the poor*. New York: Academic Press.

Goldstein, A. P., & Stein, N. (1976). *Prescriptive psychotherapies*. New York: Pergamon Press.

Hess, R. D., & Shipman, V. C. (1965). Early experience and the socialization of cognitive modes in children. *Child Development, 36,* 869-886.

Jensen, A. R. (1967). Social class and verbal learning. In J. P. DeCecco (Ed.), *The psychology of language, thought and instruction*. New York: Holt.

Joyce, B. R., & Hodges, R. E. (1966). Instructional flexibility training. *Journal of Teacher Education, 17,* 409-416.

Kiesler, D. (1966). Some myths of psychotherapy research and the search for a paradigm. *Psychological Bulletin, 65,* 110-136.

Luborsky, L., Singer, B., & Luborsky, L. (1975). Comparative studies of psychotherapies. *Archives of General Psychiatry, 32,* 995-1008.

McGinnis, E., & Goldstein, A. P. (1984). *Skillstreaming the elementary school child*. Champaign, IL: Research Press.

Melzhoff, J., & Kornriech, M. (1970). *Research in psychotherapy*. New York: Atherton.

Rachman, S. J., & Wilson, G. T. (1980). *The effects of psychological therapy*. New York: Pergamon Press.

Schofield, N. (1964). *Psychotherapy: The purchase of friendship*. Englewood Cliffs, NJ: Prentice Hall.

Schroeder, H. M., Driver, M., & Streufert, S. (1967). *Human information processing*. New York: Holt, Rinehart & Winston.

Smith, M. L., & Glass, G. V. (1977). Meta-analysis of psychotherapy outcome studies. *American Psychologist, 32,* 752-760.

Yamamoto, J., & Goin, M. K. (1965). On the treatment of the poor. *American Journal of Psychiatry, 122,* 267-271.

# The Spiritual/Religious Dimension Of Counseling: A Multicultural Perspective

*Judith G. Miranti*

### Overview

The spiritual and/or religious dimensions inherent in each individual could possibly be the most salient cultural identity for a client, surpassing even ethnographic, demographic or status variables. These spiritual/religious values could shape and direct one's world view which in turn could significantly influence one's attitudes and behaviors. For example, the lifestyle, customs, traditions, education, etc. of the Amish Community would be their most salient curtural identity. This way of life defines and demonstrates the totality of their belief system and is easily identifiable to those not espousing that particular tradition.

### Unique Problems

The practice of incorporating the spiritual dimension into counseling has as its precursor Carl Jung who is credited with introducing this dimension into Western psychology (Chandler, Holden, & Kolander, 1992). Emphasis on the use of the wellness, developmental model rather than on the use of the medical model has established a unique identity which differentiates the counseling profession from other human service professions. In so doing, counseling for spiritual wellness has become an emerging area of interest among counseling professionals. The unique problems inherent in the application of this forgotten dimension come from either a lack of clarity in defining spirituality and religion or from difficulties in incorporating this dimension into the counseling process.

### Belief System and World View

Currently, the worldview of most counselors does not include the spiritual dimension either because counselors fear being unethical by imposing their own spiritual or religious values or from a lack of their being comfortable with their own spirituality. This forgotten dimension is receiving national attention (Burke & Miranti, 1995) as evidenced by the number of workshops/ seminars addressing spirituality at national and state conventions.

Incorporating the spiritual or religious values of clients from a multicultural perspective is not only plausible but is also necessary since culture influences the way in which an individual defines self. The importance of this multicultural perspective, goes beyond the needs of any culturally or spiritually defined interest group, such as the Association for Spiritual, Ethical and Religious Values In Counseling, and the Association for Multicultural Counseling and Development, etc. (Pedersen, 1990). To some extent, all counseling is multicultural combining the individual's many different social, economic, and status roles to construct his or her basic identity. Understanding and respecting these differences are not only ethical mandates but are also a prerequisite to an accurate interpretation of client behaviors.

To accept the premise that the client's worldview influences behavior is to acknowledge the impact that the spiritual/religious dimension has on training, practice and research. Incorporating the spiritual dimension as an integral part of the counselor education curriculum would be to respond to the Council for Accreditation of Counseling and Related Educational Programs (CACREP) standard which specifically lists religious preference as one topic to be included in the curriculum (Pate & Bondi, 1992). If counselors are to respect "the individual rights and personal dignity of the client," (AACD, 1988: Ethical

Standards Section A.10) they must learn during their professional training to respect the importance of religion and spirituality in the lives of clients and how to incorporate that respect into their practice. Counselor educators must address their own level of comfort in order to incorporate into counselor training the multicultural perspective if counselors are truly to serve ethnically, racially, culturally, and religiously diverse populations.

The multicultural perspective in counseling encompasses a broad view of culture. Included in this perspective are ethnographic variables such as religion, nationality, ethnicity, and language; demographic variables such as gender, age, and locale; and status variables such as social, economic, and educational factors and affiliations (Pedersen, 1990). Coughlin (1992) reported that social scientists are showing increased interest in cultural diversity and ethnicity, and "religion is understood to be intimately tied to ethnic identity" (p.6).

The 1991 special issue on Multicultural Diversity of the *Journal of Counseling and Development* containes 11 articles which specifically include religion in the discussion of multicultural components of counseling. The importance of religion and spiritual values in counseling is likewise described by Lee (1991) in his discussion of the role of cultural dynamics in multicultural counseling.

### Implications for Training, Practice, and Research

Some practical reasons are cited for incorporating the spiritual dimension of counseling:

1. It provides the practitioner a type of metaphor or roadmap for better understanding the worldview of the client;
2. The pervasive influence of culture inclusive of spiritual and/or religious values makes the multicultural perspective a powerful fourth force in counseling (Pedersen 1990);
3. Cultural awareness and sensitivity are imperative in all counseling and affect client behaviors (Pate & Bondi, 1992);
4. Religious identity is often as strongly influencial as either racial or cultural identity;

(Worthington, 1989); and

5. The multicultural perspective includes variables such as religion, nationality, ethnicity, language, gender, age, locale, social, economic and educational factors and affiliations (Pedersen, 1990).

While counselor educators are beginning to give serious attention to the necessity for multicultural training, few are reluctant to accept the spiritual dimension from a multicultural perspective. The search for meaning and spiritual integration is as dynamic and ongoing as the search for truth (Miranti & Burke, 1992). For counselor educators, the challenge in this millennium is not whether the cultural dimension of spirituality or religious expression should be addressed in training but rather how best can this dimension be infused across the curriculum. Two recent volumes edited by Burke and Miranti (1992, 1995) chronicles the necessity for incorporating spiritual dimensions into the counseling process.

In practice, the ethical counselor recognizes and accepts the religious values and spiritual dimension of clients as he or she would accept any other unique attributes contributing to their worldview. Guided by ethical principles, practitioners are exhorted to gain knowledge, personal awareness and sensitivity and to incorporate culturally relevant practices into their work (ACA, 1994). Just as one's culture provides a comprehensive understanding of the many different perspectives taken by the individual, the professional counselor also gains an insight into these different perspectives and attempts to integrate these differences into the holistic process. Burke and Miranti (1992) view ethics and spirituality as the prevailing forces influencing the counseling process.

In his national survey of 525 counselor education programs, in which he examined the role of religion and spirituality in counselor education, Kelly (1994) reported that a minority of programs included religious and spiritual issues. Survey respondents, mostly heads of programs, considered these issues to be important. This leaves a significant gap in training.

To date, little research is available on what happens when the spiritual/religious dimension is incorporated into counseling. Researchers have examined the religious client or religious counselor, but few have attempted to examine the effects of religious counseling interventions. This presents a challenge to professional counselors to conduct high-quality research in order to investigate whether different techniques are more appropriate than others, how individuals develop spiritually across the lifespan, what religious issues people bring to counseling, etc. At present, there is no known theoretical framework to focus and guide research (Worthington, 1989).

Worthington (1989) contends in many instances that ethnic and religious identity are intertwined. He gives an example of a young adult reared in a strongly fundamentalist environment who is anxious about revealing his or her religious beliefs in secular counseling. The counselor, minimally, should ask directly whether the client attributes any role to religion in the client's perception of the causes and possible resolution of his or her problems. Such a direct question at least raises the possibility that religious issues should be addressed in order to accurately assess and properly intervene in the counseling process.

There are clients whose religious beliefs will determine their expectations about the type of counseling they will receive, their role in counseling, and the modality that will be used in counseling. For example, imagine a very religious, highly committed client who desires "Christian counseling." His or her expectations may be that the counselor is also a Christian and that the client's role will be one of deference to the authority of the counselor. The client may expect procedures similar to the ones used in his or her church, such as, Christian readings outside of the sessions, or scripture readings during sessions. The client may expect the counselor to hold the same religious beliefs as those expressed in the teachings of his or her religion. If the client thinks that certain actions are prohibited by the church, he or she may be scandalized if the counselor does not uphold that church's teaching.

## Case Study

A woman in her early thirties was referred to a licensed professional counselor for marital counseling. This client, when asking for a referral, specifically requested a counselor who was of the same religious tradition. The referring professional knew of the professional counselor's religious affiliation since they had served together on an educational advisory committee of a church-affiliated private school.

In the initial session the client made it known that she was a practicing Catholic and that it was critical that she see a counselor of the same religious tradition. She went on to state the reasons why she was in critical need of counseling. Her husband of 15 years had been having her wear different items of clothing before engaging in sex. While she did not particularly like this, she said she did so in order to please him. One day, unexpectedly, she walked into their bedroom and found him masturbating and cross-dressing. She reported that she was "devastated." Throughout the session she asked the counselor if she approved of her husband's "deviant" behaviors. The counselor knew that it was important to remain non-judgmental and, at the same time, refrain from "scandalizing" the client. The counselor was obviously in a dilemma. To affirm the client without knowing more of the marital background could possibly jeopardize the husband's coming in for counseling if he suspected that the counselor was biased against him at the outset. To not affirm the client could possibly cause a premature ending of the counseling relationship.

In order to help this client it will be necessary to incorporate the client's religious values into the counseling process while at the same time not imposing the counselor's religious values. The problems encountered in this marital relationship have strong religious implications and a successful outcome would be contingent upon the sensitivity of the professional counselor.

## Summary

Incorporating the spiritual and/or religious values of clients into the counseling process from a multicultural perspective enables the counselor to address all dimensions of the client's basic identity. While counselor educators see a need to incorporate this forgotten dimension, there are no current models available to guide and direct them in this effort. Limited outcomes research on the effects of incorporating the spiritual/religious dimension is available to counseling practitioners. There is a need to develop an infusion model similar to the one used in Gerontological Counseling which would assist counselor educators and trainees in addressing the spiritual/religious values of clients.

## References

American Association for Counseling and Development. (1988). *Ethical Standards.* Alexandria, VA: Author.

American Counseling Association. (1994). Ethical standards. *Counseling Today, 21-28.*

Burke, M. T., & Miranti, J. G. (Eds). (1995). *Counseling: The spiritual dimension.* Alexandria, VA: American Counseling Association.

Burke, M. T., & Miranti, J. G. (Eds.). (1992). *Ethical and spiritual values in counseling.* Alexandria, VA: AACD

Chandler, C. K., Holden, J. M., & Kolander, C. A. (1992). Counseling for spiritual wellness: Theory and practice. *Journal of Counseling and Development, 71,* 168-175.

Coughlin, E. K. (1992). Social scientists again turn attention to religion's place in the world. *The Chronicle of Higher Education.* pp. 6, A7. A8.

Kelly, E. W. (1994). The role of religion and spirituality in counselor education: A national survey. *Counselor Education and Supervision, 33,* 227-237.

Lee, C. C. (1991). Cultural Dynamics: Their importance in multicultural counseling, in C. C. Lee & B. L. Richardson (Eds.), *Multicultural issues in counseling: New approaches in diversity* (p.11-17). VA: AACD Press.

Miranti, J. G. & Burke, M. T. (1992). Ethics and spirituality: The prevailing forces influencing the counseling profession. In M.T. Burke & J. G. Miranti (Eds.), *Ethical and spiritual values in counseling* (p.1-4). Alexandria, VA: AACD Press.

Pate, R. H., & Bondi, A. M. (1992). Religious beliefs and practice: An integral aspect of mlticultural awareness. *Counselor Education and Supervision, 32,* 108-115.

Pedersen, P. (1989).The multicultural perspective. *Journal of Mental Health Counseling, 12,* 93-95.

Pedersen, P. (1990). Multiculturalism as a fourth force in counseling. *Journal of Mental Health Counseling, 12,* 93-95.

Worthington, E. L. (1989). Religious faith across the lifespan: Implications for counseling and research. *The Counseling Psychologist,* 17, (4) 555-612.

# Conclusion

*Paul Pedersen and Don Locke*

From the client's point of view, the discussion about cultural and diversity issues is overshadowed by the need to receive quality care when they require it. These chapters on cultural and diversity issues demonstrate the importance of the client and the client's special viewpoint in each idiographic clinical setting. It is the client's identity which is being trivialized and minimalized by an overshadowing, presumed dominant, identity reflected by the majority of counseling providers.

Leonard's chapter on African American women points out that they experience multiple discrimination because of their gender and their ethnicity. The stressors of poverty and multiple roles are the "ravaging social, psychological and economic byproducts of racism and gender bias." More research is needed to describe and explain the psychological functioning, career aspirations, and coping modalities for this special population.

American Indian and Alaska Natives are in danger of being "museumized" in the mind of the dominant culture according to LaFromboise and Young. The erosion of traditional roles by modernization has been particularly threatening to the family as a core sociocultural foundation of society. Family focused interventions may provide a positive vehicle for counseling and many Indian tribal groups are developing their own indigenous counseling strategies for social support.

Wittmer introduces the problems of the Amish as an ethnic group, whose values of peace and humility have subjected them to discrimination. All attempts to integrate, include, and invade this group by outsiders have been destructive to that basic cultural foundation. This background of persecution by outsiders presents difficult problems for the non-Amish counselor working with an Amish client.

Garland identifies the Southern Appalachian peoples as still another group victimized by outsiders who impose negative stereotypes on this population. Here again the model of the Southern Appalachians as an "ethnic group" helps legitimize their unique identity in the larger context. More attention needs to focus on indigenous support systems and particularly on the family as an essential foundation of successful counseling.

Pier's description of the Chamorro continues the theme of ethnic group uniqueness by describing the place of the family, respect, shame and relation to the cultural group. Chamorros are presented as a resourceful and resilient people whose culture must be understood by counselors if they are to be effective providers of services. She also describes comprehensive programs for working with Chamorros with implications for counseling practice.

Leong and Chou describe how Chinese American stereotypes, such as exotic, unassimilable, and immoral at worst, and law-abiding, quiet, intelligent, and hardworking at best, are hurtful. The interconnection of mind and body becomes essential to successful counseling. The medium- and low-acculturation Chinese Americans are most likely to need modifications of standard counseling procedures as a group caught in-between. More work is needed to understand the needs of medium-and low-acculturation Chinese Americans.

Salvador emphasizes the importance of counselors knowing the Filipino culture, psychosocial characteristics, cultural needs, and unique challenges before counseling American Filipino clients. The Filipino culture is a blend of Southeast and East Asian cultures, plus Spanish and American colonial influence. Not only are Filipino's culturally distinct, but there is a colonial heritage of subjugation that must also be dealt with.

Gaughen and Gaughen focus on the Native Hawaiian culture which is also unique among American indigenous peoples. The authors use the Minority Identity Development model to understand this culture in transition in terms of its cultural identity and of the political oppression by the dominant American culture. Here again the family becomes the mediating variable for successful counseling.

Gonzales describes how the profoundly differentiated group labeled as "Hispanics" actually incorporates all Spanish-speaking minorities including Latinos, Cubans, Caribbean Islanders, as well as Castilians, Mexican Americans, and others. Gonzales describes the problems of poverty as more serious than cultural differences for this group generally and presents the family as an essential foundation for mediating successful counseling.

Fukuyama describes the problems of counseling Japanese Americans due to cultural differences and political oppression during the Second World War. Each generation of Japanese Americans has its own unique identity and perspective; assimilation is nigh impossible since Japanese Americans are separated from and excluded by the dominant culture for social economic and political animosity.

Kim describes Korean Americans as one of the largest Asian American populations but one which is often overlooked. Korean Americans share many values with other Asian Americans but also have a unique cultural identity. Family values form a microcosm of harmony and are fundamental to their culture, as such values are in many of the other ethnicities. For Korean Americans the church has served a uniquely important role as a focus of their new developing identity.

College students from Taiwan are described by Lin as singular both in their temporary residence abroad and in their primary affiliation to their home culture in Taiwan. This student population is required to maintain both their back-home role in their culture of origin and their temporary student role, which rewards the accommodation of host-culture values. Balancing these often contradictory roles can be a difficult task.

White Racism, as described by D'Andrea, is based on the assumption that racism is a learned response, resulting from interacting with one's environment and all other cultural identities. By controlling the influence of racism it is possible for a counselor to change her or his role relative to other different or "non-White" cultural identities.

While this brief sample of ethnographic cultural identities is not comprehensive, it does reveal patterns of similarity. The sense of disaffiliation or exclusion was frequently mentioned as a source of stress. The importance of family as a coping resource was a constant theme, as were the exploitation of minorities by a dominant White majority culture and the range of responses to that exploitation. The difficulty that a counselor from the dominant culture faces in providing help to members of the minority ethnographic groups is overwhelming. At the same time, the necessity for all ethnic groups, including the White dominant culture, to achieve harmony and a constructive role toward one another emerges clearly as a survival issue for all of us.

The diversity populations described in Part II resemble ethnographic groups in many ways. They too report a sense of exclusion or being set apart and there is typically a sense of being exploited by more powerful dominant groups in some way. These diversity groups resemble cultures in many functional features of a shared identity, a potential salience in a given time and place, separate rules of behavior, sometimes even a separate language, and always a cohesive perspective separating insiders from outsiders. It may be useful to treat these diversity groups defined by demographic, status or affiliation "as if" they were cultures in every sense that the ethnographic groups are cultures so that we can understand the special viewpoint of clients from within each of these diversity perspectives as they approach counseling.

Petipas, Brewer and Van Raalte focus on athletes as a special population, both revered and derogated, by simplistic stereotypes. The demands of maintaining one's athletic role impose stressors on top of normal developmental controversies and—for those athletes from minority backgrounds—other ethnographic constraints. The physical, psychological, and social demands of maintaining the role of an athlete, generate highly specialized problems that require uniquely suited counseling strategies.

Nochi and Handley describe the distinctive cultural perspective of people with traumatic brain injury (TBI) confounded by physical and/or mental limitations not experienced by others. These similar experiences frequently bring the "survivors" together in a sense of community. Counselors from the outside seeking to reach this population need to work from within the client's perspective in ways that will be very difficult without specialized training.

Murgatroyd examines the particular socio-religious perspective of Buddhist clients, as both a system of beliefs and as rules for social conduct. The Buddhist perspective is defined, in contrast to the prevailing Western viewpoint, in its emphasis on interdependent and connected relationships, indirect communication styles, tolerant and accepting problem solving styles, and other strategies which are devalued in Western cultures.

Snyder describes children as an age-related group with its own cultural identity. With increased global cohesion it may be that youth share more with youth from other countries than they do with other generations within their own culture. It is clear that peer influence is a powerful force among children; adults seeking to penetrate the world of children encounter a formidable barrier.

Marshall describes disability as a unique perspective requiring training for counselors working within that perspective. Simplistic solutions have not worked and have, in fact, tended to deny the relevance of the disability. The necessity to open a dialogue and learn from more successful programs is a clear and powerful necessity.

Lorion, Holland, and Myers identify economic status as an "add-on" identity that typically confounds all of the other cultural groups as a superordinate issue. The seriousness of the problem and the limitations of coping alternatives is profoundly influenced by economic considerations. SES is not an invariant characteristic and interacts in complicated ways with other identities. To ignore the importance of economic status is to confound the difficulty in working with other cultural roles.

Nosworthy and Fajardo find cultural identity among clients who are HIV infected, thus forming a relatively new cultural affiliation. This group is defined as much by exclusion from outsiders as by internal cohesion. In responding to external pressures anddemands, the HIV infected client has learned to take on new rules and a new identity that overshadows previous cultural affiliations. The special problems of an outsider counselor working with HIV infected clients are profound.

Daniels looks at homelessness particularly as it shapes the cultural identity of children and their families. People without a "place" or "home" of their own lose an important resource on which counseling often depends. Usually, people who are homeless also experience confounding social, political, economic, and ethnic pressures as well. The rapid increase in this group presents urgent problems to those seeking to provide meaningful counseling services.

Deen describes one international population in the Netherlands as an example of the difficulty experienced in providing counseling services abroad. Looking at how immigrants and refugees have been accommodated in the Netherlands demonstrates both the similarities and the differences of counseling abroad. While the counselors need the same self-awareness, other-awareness, and ability to avoid stereotypes in working with conflicting value systems, the constraints in each cultural or in international settings also require study.

Browning identifies Lesbian, Gay, and Bisexual groups as having their own cultural identity. Until recently, these roles have been treated as a pathology, making the stereotype particularly destructive. This identity is frequently invisible, especially to outsiders, which presents unique problems in itself. Stages in the development of a lesbian, gay, or bisexual identity are complicated and are dependent on unifying experiences within the group, as well as interaction with outsiders.

Bemak describes refugees as being forced into

a cultural identity by socio-political-economic forces beyond their control. The experience of helplessness is particularly stressful for this population, especially when working with counselors who could not possibly understand what the refugee has experienced.

Richard Pearson and Beverly Burnell describe the rural client as having a unique identity. They examine four issues which cut across geographic and personlogical variables: isolation, the primacy of face-to-face exchange, the importance of place, and a pragmatic view of helping and change. These factors can serve as useful reference points to counselors and other helping professionals when working with clients who have been shaped by rural life.

Goldstein describes social class as imposing its own rules for prescriptive intervention by counselors. The need to avoid the "one true light" perspective in dealing with social class issues is clear in the many failures counseling has demonstrated. While social class provides a unified identity, it is not unimodal and must be customized for each individual client in a "many true lights" contrasting perspective.

Miranti describes the spiritual/religious dimension of counseling as imposing still another unique perspective. Religion provides the underlying core beliefs of each cultural affiliation and can not be avoided regardless of the cultures being served. By approaching the culture through this spiritual/religious dimension, it is sometimes possible to enter into the client's own special worldview.

### Conclusion

Several patterns have emerged in this examination of cultural and diversity issues for counseling which weave the threads of arguments together in a cloth of understanding. To use another metaphor, the overlapping rings of influence each cultural identity imposes on all other identities necessitates a complex and dynamic perspective on the presumptuousness of any counselor seeking to serve a multicultural population.

I. While each of the groups discussed had its own unique identity, that identity was never unimodal and was always confounded by within-group differences that disallow stereotypes.

2. Each group typically had problems with "outsiders", coming in to serve and help, who did not already belong and/or were unwilling to approach the client from within that client's own worldview.

3. There is typically a socio-political-economic aspect to the cultural affiliation—particularly in relation to a dominant culture—which is based in history and which can not be changed.

4. There is typically an emotional quality to the cultural identity which may become more important than the rational arguments for or against what any counselor might advise.

5. Each of the cultural groups is dynamic and not static, changing constantly for each individual in each situation and at different rates over time, thus presenting a moving target for even the well-trained counselor.

6. Implicit stereotypes which label the member with an adjective—such as the special individual—are typically less accurate than designating the individual first—such as the individual who happens to be special.

7. The complexity of thousands of potentially salient cultural identities competing for attention is present in every counseling situation and not just those where the cultural affiliation is most obvious.

8. The primitive level of training to prepare counselors to work with this complicated cultural identity of their clients will require immediate attention.

9. Ethnographic, demographic, status, and affiliation variables of each client's identity are interactive and can not be dealt with separately.

10. There are important resources, such as

the family and collectivity, which can be mobilized to provide within-group support in the healing process we call counseling.

There are many lessons to be learned in the study of cultural and diversity issues of counseling. The lesson is urgently and profoundly important for all counselors to prepare them for accurate assessment, meaningful understanding, and appropriate interventions as counselors.

# Biographies

Fred Bemak is an Associate Professor and Chair in the Department of Counseling and Human Services at The Johns Hopkins University. Dr. Bemak is a former Fulbright Scholar, Kellogg International Fellow and recipient of the International Exchange of Experts Fellowship through the World Rehabilitation Fund. He has been working nationally with refugees for the past 13 years as a researcher, clinician, and clinical consultant and is currently working on a book with Rita Chi-Ying Chung, Paul Pedersen, and Thomas Bornemann entitled *Multicultural Counseling with Refugees: A Case Study Approach to Innovative Interventions.*

Britton W. Brewer, Ph.D., is an Assistant Professor of Psychology at the Center for Performance Enhancement and Applied Research at Springfield College, Springfield, MA.

Christine Browning, Ph.D. is a staff psychologist at the University of California Counseling Center, Irvine, CA and in private practice. She is a member of the APA Committee on Lesbian and Gay Concerns and has served on the Executive Board of the APA Division on the Psychological Study of Gay and Lesbian Issues (Division 44) and the Association of Lesbian and Gay Psychologists.

Beverly A. Burnell is a doctoral candidate in Counselor Education at Syracuse University.

Michael D'Andrea is an associate professor in the Department of Counselor Education at the University of Hawaii.

Judy Daniels received her Ed.D. from the Peabody College of Vanderbilt University. She is currently an Associate Professor in the Department of Counselor Education at the University of Hawai'i, Manoa. Dr. Daniels co-founded and subsequently became the fist president of both the Hawai'i Association for Multicultural Counseling and development and the Hawai'i Association for Counselor Education and Supervision.

Nathan Deen is professor of guidance and counseling at Utrecht University, the Netherlands. He has worked as a teacher educator, curriculum developer, and researcher at the Kohnstamm-Institute for Educational Research at Amsterdam University, and served for some years as the director of that Institute. He developed the first Counselor Education program in the Netherlands, which has served as a model for subsequent programs and founded the *International Journal for the Advancement of Counselling.*

Eva Fajardo is a licensed mental health counselor and certified addictions specialist in private practice in Orlando, Florida.

Mary A. Fukuyama, Ph.D., is Professor and Counseling Psychologist at the University of Florida Counseling Center, Gainesville, Florida. Her professional interests include multicultural and spiritual issues in counseling.

Hettie Lou Garland is a native of Southern Appalachia, born in Bakersville, NC. She is Director, Division of Regional Education Programs at the Mountain Area Health Education Center in Asheville, N.C. She is a student in the N C. State University Doctoral Program in Adult and Community College Education at The Asheville Graduate Center.

Kiaka J. S. Gaughen is a graduate student in the Department of Counselor Education at the University of Hawai'i.

Dorothy K. Gaughen is an undergraduate student in the Department of Psychology at the University of Hawai'i.

Arnold P. Goldstein, Ph.D. (Clinical Psychology, Penn State, 1959), is the developer of three increasingly comprehensive approaches to prosocial skills training, *Skillstreaming* (Goldstein, 1980), *Aggression Replacement Training* (Goldstein & Glick, 1987), and *The Prepare Curriculum* (Goldstein, 1988). In doing so, his joint concern has been curriculum development and evaluation, as well as devising instructional techniques for the purpose of effective training.

Gerardo M. Gonzalez is Associate Dean of the College of Education at the University of Florida. From 1989 to 1993 he served as Chairperson of the Department of Counselor Education at the University of Florida. Dr. Gonzalez is active in multicultural counseling and educational issues. He has addressed national and international groups and has published scholarly works on the Cuban-American experience and Hispanic educational concerns.

Mary Handley is a doctoral candidate in rehabilitation counseling program at Syracuse University. She is a certified rehabilitation counselor who has 10 years experience in traumatic brain injury rehabilitation.

Cheryl Cole Holland, MA, is a doctoral candidate in Clinical/Community Psychology at the University of Maryland and predoctoral intern in psychology at The National Children's Medical Center, Washington, DC. Her research examines environmental and individual factors that contribute to the occurrence of early childhood disorder.

Bryan S. K. Kim earned a Master of Education degree with an emphasis in counseling and Guidance from the University of Hawaii in May 1995. Mr. Kim is currently a counselor/therapist at the Hawaii Counseling and Education Center. He is also the Vice President of Hawaii Multicultural Counseling and Development Association.

Don C. Locke is Director of the North Carolina State University doctoral program in Adult and Community Education at the Asheville Graduate Center. He is the author or co-author of more than 60 publications, with a current focus on multicultural issues. He has been active in state, regional, and national organizations. He earned his doctorate at Ball State University in 1974.

Raymond P. Lorion, Ph.D., is Professor of Psychology and Director of Clinical/Community Psychology at the University of Maryland and Adjunct Professor of Mental Hygiene at the School of Hygiene and Public Health, The Johns Hopkins University. He researches factors that contribute to risks and protection for emotional and behavioral disorders and to the design and evaluation of interventions to reduce disorder and promote health.

Catherine A. Marshall, Ph.D. is the Director of Research, American Indian Rehabilitation Research and Training Center, Northern Arizona University, Flagstaff, Arizona

Judith G. Miranti, Ed.D. is a professor of Counselor Education and is the Dean of Graduate Studies at Our Lady of Holy Cross College in New Orleans, Louisiana. Judith has been a practicing Marriage and Family Counselor for the past 12 years and has incorporated the spiritual/religious values into the counseling process. She is a past president of the Association for Religious and Spiritual values in Counseling now the Association for Spiritual, Ethical, and Religious Values in Counseling (ASERVIC).

Wanpen Murgatroyd is an assistant professor in the counseling graduate program at the University of New Orleans.

Tracy Myers, MA, is a doctoral candidate in Clinical/Community Psychology at the University of Maryland and predoctoral intern at the Veteran's Hospital, Baltimore Maryland. His research examines ethnic and ecological factors (including community violence and parenting practices) which contribute to risk for emotional disorder in inner-city youth.

Masahiro Nochi is a doctoral candidate in the rehabilitation counseling program at Syracuse University. He has been researching cognitive rehabilitation for several years in Japan.

Kathryn L. Norsworthy is a licensed psychogist and an Assistant Professor in Graduate Studies in Counseling, Rollins College, Winter Park, Florida.

Richard E. Pearson is a Professor of Counselor Education at Syracuse University, Syracuse, NY.

Paul B. Pedersen is a Professor in the Department of Human Studies at the University of Alabama-Birmingham. He has been a university faculty member at the University of Minnesota, the University of Hawaii, and Syracuse University as well as for six years in Indonesia, Malaysia and Taiwan. He has published 26 books, 44 chapters and 76 articles on various aspects of multicultural counseling and communication.

Albert J. Petitpas, Ed.D., is Professor of Psychology at the Center for Performance Enhancement and Applied Research at Springfield College, Springfield, MA.

Beverly A. Snyder received her Ed.D. in Educational Leadership from the University of Central Florida. She is an assistant professor in the Department of Counseling & Human Resources at The University of Colorado at Colorado Springs. She is licensed as a community and mental health counselor in several states and is also a NCC. She maintains a limited private practice and specializes in play therapy with children and families.

Judy L. Van Raalte, Ph.D., is an Associate Professor of Psychology at the Center for Performance Enhancement and Applied Research at Springfield College, Springfield, MA.

Joe Wittmer, Ph.D., is Distinguished Service Professor and Chair, Counselor Education Department, University of Florida, Gainesville

Kate E. Young received her Master's Degree in Counseling Psychology from LesleyCollege in 1993. She is now a doctoral student in Counseling Psychology at Stanford University. Her main research interests include the effects of trauma—particularly sexual abuse—on individuals, groups, and communities; the identity development of people who have been victimized; recovery from trauma; the treatment of trauma; and multicultural counseling.

# ERIC/CASS
# Resources

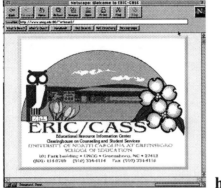

# ERIC/CASS Website

**University of
North Carolina at
Greensboro
School of Education
101 Park Building    UNCG
Greensboro, NC 27412**

**http://www.uncg.edu/~ericcas2**

One of the best sources of educational information is ERIC—the Educational Resources Information Center. An appropriate first step in gaining access to ERIC is to locate the ERIC/CASS Website and through it identify a multitude of educational resources. Numerous "hotlinks" to other databases and websites can also be reached through the ERIC/CASS Website.

Through ERIC/CASS, the U.S. Department of Education's extensive educational resources can be accessed as well as special services of the ERIC system (AskERIC, Access ERIC and other ERIC Clearinghouses). Among the specific resources available on the ERIC/CASS Website are:

- Search capability of the ERIC database through the U.S. Department of Education
- Information on forthcoming ERIC/CASS Listservs
- Access to other members of the Counselor and Therapist Support System— CATS[2] :
  - National Association of School Psychologists
  - National Board of Certified Counselors
  - National Career Development Association
  - American Psychological Association—School Directorate
  - Canadian Guidance & Counseling Foundation
- Full text ERIC/CASS Digests
- Information on forthcoming conferences and workshops
- Shopping mall of publications and resources

For more information on ERIC/CASS, call (910) 334-4114, FAX (910) 334-4116, e-mail: ericcas@hamlet.uncg.edu, or access the ERIC/CASS Homepage at:

### http://www.uncg.edu/~ericcas2.

# ERIC Counseling and Student Services Clearinghouse

*What is ERIC/CASS?*

Located around the country, ERIC Clearinghouses are responsible for acquiring, processing, and disseminating information about a particular aspect or subject area of education, such as the ERIC Counseling and Student Services aearinghouse (ERIC/CASS, formerly ERIC Counseling and Personnel Services, ERIC/CAPS) at the University of North Carolina at Greensboro.

The ERIC Counseling and Student Services aearinghouse (ERIC/CASS) was one of the original clearinghouses established in 1966 by Dr. Garry R. Walz at The University of Michigan and has been in continuous operation since that date. Its scope area includes school counseling, school social work, school psychology, mental health counseling, marriage and family counseling, career counseling, and student development, as well as parent, student, and teacher education in the human services area. Topics covered by ERIC/CASS include: the training, supervision, and continuing professional development of counseling' student services, student development, and human services professionals; counseling theories, methods, and practices; the roles of counselors, social workers, and psychologists in all educational settings at all educational levels; career planning and development; self-esteem and self-efficacy; marriage and family counseling; and mental health services to special populations such as substance abusers, pregnant teenagers, students at risk, public offenders, etc.

## *What can ERIC/CASS do for me?*

*1. We can help you find the information you need.*

Whether we help you to use the print indexes, (RIE and CIJE), an on-line search service, or ERIC on CD-ROM, our expertise in retrieving information related to counseling and human services can help you locate a wealth of material related to your particular area of interest. You can learn more about ERIC/CASS services be telephoning CASS for further information.

*2. We can provide you with high quality, low-cost resources.*

Ranging from two-page information digests to in-depth monographs and books of readings, ERIC/CASS publications have proved to be highly valuable resources that you can use for your own personal or professional development. CASS video has proved to be extremely well-received because of its focus on topics of high interest, its "realist" flavor, and its low cost.

## *Now do I contact ERIC/CASS?*

Address:  ERIC Counseling and Student Services Clearinghouse
School of Education
University of North Carolina at Greensboro
Greensboro, NC 27412-5001

Phone: (919) 334-4114                Fax: (919) 334-4116
Website: http://www.uncg.edu/~ericcas2

ERIC/CASS exists to serve anyone who has a need to access information related to counseling and student services. We are funded by the U.S. Department of Education's Office of Educational Research and Improvement and the School of Education of the University of North Carolina at Greensboro. We encourage you to contact us with your questions and concerns. Our goal is to provide professional service and quality information to all users.

# The ERIC Information System

## *What is ERIC?*

ERIC (Educational Resources Information Center) is a national information system that provides ready access to an extensive body of education-related literature. Through its 16 subject-specific clearinghouses and four support components, ERIC provides a variety of services and products including acquiring and indexing documents and journal articles, producing publications, responding to requests, and distributing microfilmed materials to libraries nation-wide. In addition, ERIC maintains a database of over 800,000 citations to documents and journal articles.

## *Why is ERIC important?*

ERIC print or database products are available at over 3,000 locations world-wide as the most widely-used education database. Approximately 900 of these locations maintain complete microfiche collections of ERIC documents and provide search services for clients. ERIC is the most popular on-line database used in public libraries, the second-most popular in research and university libraries, and the third-most popular overall. On CD-ROM, ERIC is the most popular database in public libraries and information centers throughout the world. Above all, ERIC has committed itself to reaching audiences that include practitioner, policymakers, and parents.

## *How are information requests handled?*

Responses to information requests include:
- Send requested printed materials or answer questions (e.g., providing materials on exemplary programs or practices, instructional methods or curricular materials; explaining eclucation terms or "hot topics");

- Search the ERIC database or the reference and referral databases; and

- Refer the inquirer to other federal, national or local resource centers.

## *How do I learn more about ERIC?*

ACCESS ERIC is a toll-free service to keep clients informed of the wealth of education informal on offered by ERIC and other sources. ACCESS ERIC staff answer questions, refer callers to educational sources, provide infortnation about the ERIC network, and produce the free publications *A Pocket Guide to ERIC* and *All About ERIC*. The toll-free telephone number for ACCESS ERIC is 1-800 LET-ERIC.

Summarized from *Myths and Realities about ERIC* by Robert M. Stonehill, an ERIC Digest (EDO-IR-92) developed by the ERIC Clearinghouse on Information Resources at Syracuse University, Syracuse, NY, June 1992.

# DOCUMENT DELIVERY

**ERIC**®

## How To Get *DOCUMENTS* Announced By ERIC

Two monthly abstract/index journals announce education-related Journal Articles and Documents collected by ERIC

### *Current Index to Journals in Education* (CIJE)

Announces journal articles

### *Resources in Education* (RIE)

Announces unpublished or limited distribution documents

These two publications are available in paper form and all the citations they announce are also contained in the ERIC database, which can be accessed online or through CD-ROM. Once you identify an item you want reproduced, your options depend on whether it is a journal article or a document. Journal articles (CIJE) are identified by an EJ number. Documents (RIE) are identified by an ED number.

## Documents (ED's)—Cited in RIE

There are three principal ways to obtain documents cited in ERIC's database:
- by ordering them from the ERIC Document Reproduction Service (EDRS);
- by finding the microfiche for the document in one of the many ERIC standing order microfiche collections located at major libraries around the country and the world;
- by ordering the document from its original source or other non-ERIC suppliers noted in the ERIC citation.

### EDRS

Most documents announced in RIE can be ordered inexpensively from EDRS in either microfiche ($1.23 per title) or reproduced paper copy ($3.53 per 25 pages), plus postage. If you want to receive all documents on microfiche in regular monthly shipments, you can subscribe for about $2,000 per year. Clearly identified orders are processed within 5 days. Orders can be placed via mail, telephone, FAX, or online vendor system. An EDRS order form can be found at the back of RIE. The EDRS address is: EDRS, 7420 Fullerton Road, Suite 110, Springfield, Virginia 22153-2852. Telephone: 1-800-443-ERIC

### Standing Order Microfiche

Over 900 organizations, including most major universities, subscribe to ERIC's complete microfiche collection and are listed in the Directory of ERIC Information Service Providers (available from ACCESS ERIC), (800-LET-ERIC). Using the Directory, locate the ERIC microfiche collection geographically closest or most convenient to you. At most locations, you will be able to copy selected pages; at some locations you will be able to obtain a duplicate microfiche. This is probably the quickest way to obtain an ERIC document and has the advantage of permitting you to review a document before buying it.

### Original (Non-ERIC) Source

Some document preparers sell their product directly and, therefore, may not let ERIC reproduce it. About 5% of ERIC documents are available from their original sources (In addition to or in lieu of being available from EDRS). Full address and price information (when given) specifying such external availability is always in the ERIC citation.

# AN INVITATION TO SUBMIT DOCUMENTS TO ERIC/CASS

## *What is ERIC*

ERIC is the largest and most searched education database in the world with print or database products being distributed to over 3000 locations around the world. Each year nearly a half-million online searches of the ERIC database are conducted by over 100,000 users in 90 different countries. On CD-ROM, ERIC is the most popular database in public libraries and information centers. In addition, free access to all or part of the ERIC database through Internet is rapidly increasing.

## *What is ERIC/CASS*

ERIC/CASS is the ERIC Clearinghouse on Counseling and Student Services located at the University of North Carolina at Greensboro. One of sixteen subject-specific clearinghouses, ERIC/CASS is responsible for acquiring, processing, and disseminating information about counseling, psychology, and social work as it relates to education at all levels and in all settings.

## *Advantages of Having a Document in ERIC*
- *World-Wide Visibility*
- *Free Reproduction/Distribution*
- *Free Publicity/Marketing*
- *Timely Dissemination of Your Publication*
- *Opportunity to Disseminate Your Work in a Variety of Formats*
- *Recognition as a Refereed Publication*
- *Assurance That Your Publication Will Always Be Available*
- *Ease of Submission*
- *Freedom to Publish Elsewhere*

### *Selection Criteria Employed by ERIC*

*Quality of Content*

All documents received are evaluated by subject experts against the following kinds of quality criteria: contribution to knowledge, significance, relevance, newness, innovativeness, effectiveness of presentation, thoroughness of reporting, relation to current priorities, timeliness, authority of source, intended audience, comprehensiveness.

*Legibility and Reproducibility*

Documents may be typeset, typewritten, xeroxed, or otherwise duplicated. They must be legible and easily readable. Letters should be clearly formed and with sufficient contrast to the paper background to permit filming. Colored inks and colored papers can create serious reproduction problems. Standard 8 1/2" x 11" size pages are preferred. Two copies are desired, if possible: one for processing into the system and eventual filming, one for retention and possible use by the appropriate Clearinghouse while processing is going on. However, single copies are acceptable.

## Completed Reproduction Release

For each document accepted, ERIC must obtain a formal signed Reproduction Release form indicating whether or not ERIC may reproduce the document. A copy of the Release Form is included in this packet. Additional Release forms may be copied as needed or obtained from the ERIC Facility or any ERIC Clearinghouse. Items that are accepted, and for which permission to reproduce has been granted, will be made available in microfiche only (Level 2), or microfiche and reproduced paper copy (Level 1) by the ERIC Document Reproduction Service (EDRS). The Release form must be signed by the author or, if copyrighted, by the person or organization holding the copyright.

## Appropriate Kinds of Documents to Send ERIC

ERIC would like to be given the opportunity to examine virtually any document dealing with education or its aspects. Examples of the kinds of materials collected include:

- Research Reports/Technical Reports
- Program/Project Descriptions and Evaluations
- Opinion Papers, Essays, Position Papers
- Monographs, Treatises
- Speeches and Presentations
- State of the Art Studies
- Instructional Materials and Syllabi
- Teaching and Resource Guides
- Manuals and Handbooks
- Curriculum Materials
- Conference Papers
- Bibliographies, Annotated Bibliographies
- Legislation and Regulations
- Tests, Questionnaires, Measurement Devices
- Statistical Compilations
- Taxonomies and Classifications
- Dissertations

A document does not have to be formally published to be entered into the ERIC database. In fact, ERIC will not accept material that has been published elsewhere (e.g, journal articles, book chapters, etc.) and is readily available through public or university libraries. Rather, ERIC seeks out the unpublished or "fugitive" material *not* usually available through conventional library channels.

## Where to Send Documents

If you and/or your organization have papers or materials that meet the above criteria and you would like to submit them for possible inclusion in ERIC's Resources in Education, please send two copies and a signed Reproduction Release form for each to:

ERIC/CASS Acquisitions
School of Education
101 Park Building
University of North Carolina at Greensboro
Greensboro, NC   27412-5001

# Advantages of Having a Document in ERIC

*World-Wide Visibility*

ERIC is the largest and most searched education database in the world with print or database products being distributed to over 3000 locations around the world. Each year nearly a half-million online searches of the ERIC database are conducted by over 100,000 users in 90 different countries. On CD-ROM, ERIC is quite "user-friendly" and is the most popular database in public libraries and information centers. In addition, free access to all or part of the ERIC database through Internet is rapidly increasing.

*Free Reproduction/Distribution*

If you check the Level 1 box on the Reproduction Release form (permitting microfiche-paper copy, electronic, and optical media reproduction), the ERIC Document Reproduction Service (EDRS) will make your document available to users at no cost to you. This can mean considerable savings to you in time, postage, and copy costs if, for example, you have presented a paper at a professional conference and receive numerous requests for reprints.

*Free Publicity/Marketing*

If, on the other hand, your publication is one that you wish to sell yourself, you can check the Level 2 box on the ERIC Reproduction Release form (permitting reproduction in other than paper copy). Level 2 documents can be obtained only through the source(s) identified in the "availability" field of the RIE citation which can also specify ordering information, e.g., cost, organization address, phone number, etc. While it is technically possible for someone to make a paper copy from a microfiche reader-printer, people very seldom choose to do this because these copies are almost always less attractive and more expensive than the copies sold by the publisher.

*Early Dissemination of Your Publication*

Unlike the long delay you experience when you submit articles to journals and manuscripts to book publishers, the usual turnaround time for documents accepted for RIE is four to six months from the time the Clearinghouse receives your document.

*Opportunity to Disseminate Your Work in a Variety of Formats*

Many of the documents you produce in your professional career, e.g., program descriptions, program evaluation reports, teacher guides, student handbooks, etc., are not in a form acceptable for journal publication and may not be considered "profitable" enough for a commercial publisher to handle. Still, the information contained in these documents could be of invaluable help to someone else who is working on similar projects or ideas. ERIC provides the opportunity to share your work with others without "re-packaging it."

*Recognition as a Refereed Publication*

Documents submitted to a Clearinghouse are first reviewed for educational relevance, then for relevance to the scope of that Clearinghouse. Out-of-scope documents are transferred to the appropriate Clearinghouse for review and in-scope documents are submitted to the Clearinghouse's RIE Selection Committee. This committee, which is composed of both ERIC technical specialists and subject matter experts, reviews each document according to the criteria specified in this flyer. At the present time, approximately 32 percent of the documents submitted are rejected.

*Assurance That Your Publication Will Always Be Available*

The presence of a master microfiche at EDRS, from which copies can be made on an on demand basis, means that ERIC documents are constantly available and never go "out of print." This archival function can relieve you of the burden of maintaining copies for possible future distribution and can solve the availability problem when your supply has been exhausted.

*Ease of Submission*

To encourage submission, ERIC offers to send contributors notice of document disposition, giving the ED identification number of those documents selected for RIE. There are no fees to pay in submitting documents to ERIC, nor does ERIC pay any royalties for material it accepts. Other than the Reproduction Release which is readily available from any ERIC component, there are no forms to complete. Additionally, ERIC will send a complimentary microfiche to each contributor when the document is announced in RIE.

*Freedom to Publish Elsewhere*

While the Reproduction Release gives ERIC permission to abstract, index, and reproduce your work, no copyright is involved—you remain free to submit your work to any journal or publisher.

*This information sheet was prepared by the ERIC Clearinghouse on Counseling and Student Services at the University of North Carolina at Greensboro. If you would have questions or would like further information, please contact us at ERIC/CASS, School of Education, 101 Park Building, UNCG, Greensboro, NC, 27412, Phone: (910) 334-4114 or 1-800-414-9769.*

# REPRODUCTION RELEASE
(Specific Document)

## I. DOCUMENT IDENTIFICATION:

| | |
|---|---|
| Title: | |
| Author(s): | |
| Corporate Source: | Publication Date: |

## II. REPRODUCTION RELEASE:

In order to disseminate as widely as possible timely and significant materials of interest to the educational community, documents announced in the monthly abstract journal of the ERIC system, *Resources in Education* (RIE), are usually made available to users in microfiche, reproduced paper copy, and electronic/optical media, and sold through the ERIC Document Reproduction Service (EDRS) or other ERIC vendors. Credit is given to the source of each document, and. if reproduction release is granted, one of the following notices is affixed to the document.

If permission is granted to reproduce and disseminate the identified document, please CHECK ONE of the following two options and sign at the bottome of the page.

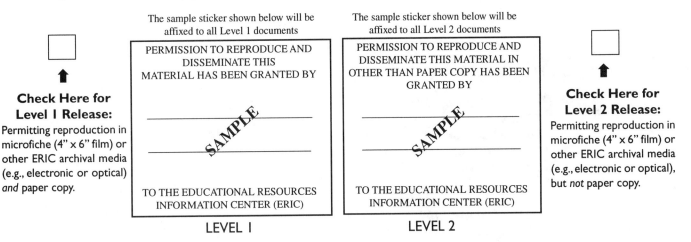

The sample sticker shown below will be affixed to all Level 1 documents

**Check Here for Level 1 Release:**
Permitting reproduction in microfiche (4" x 6" film) or other ERIC archival media (e.g., electronic or optical) *and* paper copy.

PERMISSION TO REPRODUCE AND DISSEMINATE THIS MATERIAL HAS BEEN GRANTED BY

SAMPLE

TO THE EDUCATIONAL RESOURCES INFORMATION CENTER (ERIC)

**LEVEL 1**

The sample sticker shown below will be affixed to all Level 2 documents

PERMISSION TO REPRODUCE AND DISSEMINATE THIS MATERIAL IN OTHER THAN PAPER COPY HAS BEEN GRANTED BY

SAMPLE

TO THE EDUCATIONAL RESOURCES INFORMATION CENTER (ERIC)

**LEVEL 2**

**Check Here for Level 2 Release:**
Permitting reproduction in microfiche (4" x 6" film) or other ERIC archival media (e.g., electronic or optical), but *not* paper copy.

DOCUMENTS WILL BE PROCESSED AS INDICATED PROVIDED REPRODUCTION QUALITY PERMITS. IF PERMISSION TO REPRODUCE IS GRANTED, BUT NEITHER BOX IS CHECKED, DOCUMENTS WILL BE PROCESSED AT LEVEL 1.

"I hereby grant to the Educational Resources Information Center (ERIC) nonexclusive permission to reproduce and disseminate this document as indicated above. Reproduction from the ERIC microfiche or electronic/optical media by persons other than ERIC employees and its system contractors requires permission from the copyright holder. Exception is made for non-profit reproduction by libraries and other service agencies to satisfy information needs of educators in response to discrete inquiries."

**SIGN HERE PLEASE** →

| Signature: | Printed Name/Position/Title: | |
|---|---|---|
| Organization/Address: | Telephone: | FAX: |
| | E-Mail Address: | Date: |

## III. DOCUMENT AVAILABILITY INFORMATION (FROM NON-ERIC SOURCE):

If permission to reproduce is not granted to ERIC, or, if you wish ERIC to cite the availability of the document from another source, please provide the following information regarding the availability of the document. (ERIC will not announce a document unless it is publicly available, and a dependable source can be specified. Contributors should also be aware that ERIC selection criiteria are significantly more stringent for documents that cannot be made available through EDRS.)

| | |
|---|---|
| Publisher/Distributor: | |
| Address: | |
| Price: | |

## IV. REFERRAL OF ERIC TO COPYRIGHT/REPRODUCTION RIGHTS HOLDER:

If the right to grant reproduction release is held by someone other than the addressee, please provide the appropriate name and address:

| | |
|---|---|
| Name: | |
| Address: | |

## V. WHERE TO SEND THIS FORM:

Send this form to the following ERIC Clearinghouse:

**ERIC/CASS**
**School of Education**
**101 Park Building, UNCG**
**Greensboro, NC  27412-5001**

**Telephone: 910-334-4114**
**Toll Free: 800-414-9769**
**FAX: 910-334-4116**
**e-mail: ericcas2@dewey.uncg.edu**
**Website: http://www.uncg.edu/~ericcas2**

However, if solicited by the ERIC Facility, or if making an unsolicited contribution to ERIC, return this form (and the document being contributed) to:

ERIC Processing and Reference Facility
1100 West Street, 2nd Floor
Laurel, Maryland  20707-3598

Telephone: 301-497-4080
Toll Free: 800-799-3742
FAX: 301-953-0263
e-mail: ericfac@inet.ed.gov
Website: http://ericfac.piccard.csc.com

146

# NETWORK WITH ERIC/CASS!

On a regular basis ERIC/CASS disseminates information about important topics to members of special interest and professional focus networks. Among the items distributed are newsletters, announcements of new products and resources, ERIC Digests, new releases, workshop and conference information, and updates on new developments in ERIC and information technology. If you are interested in becoming an ERIC/CASS Networker, please complete this form.

Name:

Preferred Title:  ❏ Mr.  ❏ Mrs.  ❏ Ms.  ❏ Dr.

Address: _____

_____

City: _____ State: _____ Zip: _____

Phone Numbers:
Home: _____ Office: _____ FAX: _____

Internet Address : _____

Position: _____ Level/Setting: _____

_Counselor/Therapist
_School Psychologist
_Social Worker
_Counselor Educator
_School Psych. Educator
_Social Work Educator
_Administrator
_Student
_Other _____

_ Elementary School
_ Middle/Junior High School
_ High School
_ K-12/District Office
_ Intermediate School Dist.
_ Junior/Community College
_ College/University

_ Community Agency
_ Government Agency
_ Professional Association
_ Private Practice
_ Other _____

Major Interests:

1. _____ 2. _____ 3. _____

Mail To:

*ERIC/CASS NETWORKER*
School of Education
101 Park Building
University of North Carolina at Greensboro
Greensboro, NC 27412-5001
FAX (910) 334-4116

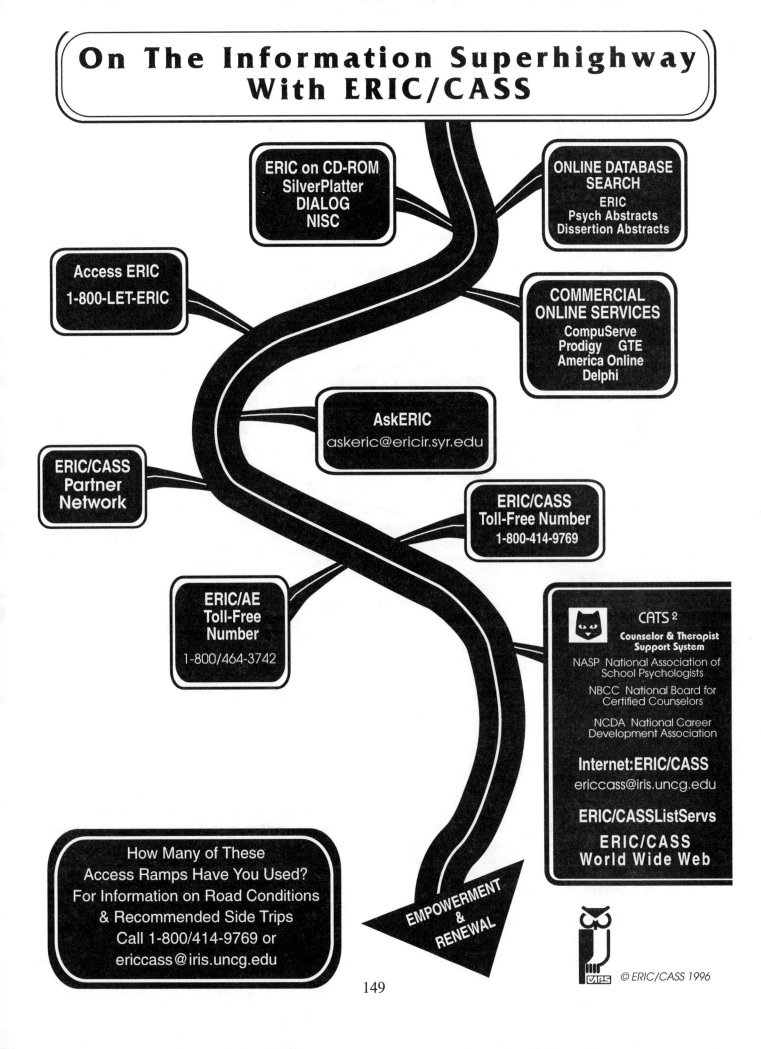

# On The Information Superhighway With ERIC/CASS

**ERIC on CD-ROM**
SilverPlatter
DIALOG
NISC

**ONLINE DATABASE SEARCH**
ERIC
Psych Abstracts
Dissertation Abstracts

**Access ERIC**
1-800-LET-ERIC

**COMMERCIAL ONLINE SERVICES**
CompuServe
Prodigy    GTE
America Online
Delphi

**AskERIC**
askeric@ericir.syr.edu

**ERIC/CASS Partner Network**

**ERIC/CASS Toll-Free Number**
1-800-414-9769

**ERIC/AE Toll-Free Number**
1-800/464-3742

**CATS²**
**Counselor & Therapist Support System**

NASP  National Association of School Psychologists

NBCC  National Board for Certified Counselors

NCDA  National Career Development Association

**Internet: ERIC/CASS**
ericcass@iris.uncg.edu

**ERIC/CASS ListServs**

**ERIC/CASS World Wide Web**

How Many of These Access Ramps Have You Used? For Information on Road Conditions & Recommended Side Trips Call 1-800/414-9769 or ericcass@iris.uncg.edu

EMPOWERMENT & RENEWAL

## ONLINE DATABASE SEARCH

Traditionally, online access to ERIC and other national databases has been available through several commercial vendors who offer sophisticated search capabilities. Because it requires training in the vendor's search language, this type of searching is usually performed by librarians and other information professionals. Online vendors include: BRS Information Technologies; Data-Star/ DIALOG Information Services; GTE Educational Network Services; and OCLC (Online Computer Library Center).

## ERIC on CD-ROM

In the mid-1980s, the vendors of the databases began to provide users with more direct access by putting the databases on CD-ROM. However, because of the expense of the hardware needed and the price of an annual subscription (>$1,000), individual users still needed to gain access via universities and libraries. An encouraging development: In 1994 Oryx Press (1-800-279-ORYX) announced the availability of CIJE on Disc for $199.00 per year; and NISC (410-243-0797) is expected to make the entire ERIC database available for approximately $100 per year early in 1995. Other CD-ROM vendors include: DIALOG (1-800-334-2564); EBSCO Publishers (1-800-653-2726); and SilverPlatter Information, Inc. (1-800-343-0064).

## COMMERCIAL ONLINE SERVICES

For individuals who do not have access to database search service or the Internet through their place of employment, one of the commercial services may be a viable alternative. Among the better known are America Online, Compuserve, and GTE Educational Network Services, all of which feature "AskERIC" information on current topics in education. Many also offer the capability of searching the ERIC database.

## Access ERIC

A component of the ERIC system that offers a central contact point for the entire system, Access ERIC disseminates general information about ERIC and responds to specific inquiries on its toll-free number (1-800-LET-ERIC).

## AskERIC

ERIC's first question-answering service offered through the Internet. Established by the ERIC Clearinghouse on Information and Technology, AskERIC now responds to thousands of online requests per week. To access AskERIC, simply send an e-mail message to AskERIC@ericir.syr.edu.
AskERIC also maintains a large gopher site for educational resources.

## ERIC/CASS Partner Network

The largest ERIC Partner network on the system, disseminates information to counseling and psychology professional associations and graduate training departments.

## ERIC/CASS Toll-Free Number

For direct access to the ERIC Clearinghouse on Counseling and Student Services, call 1-800-414-9769.

## ERIC/AE Toll-Free Number

For direct access to the ERIC Clearinghouse on Assessment and Evaluation, call 1-800-464-3742.

## Internet: ERIC/CASS

To contact ERIC/CASS via e-mail, send a message to ericcass@iris.uncg.edu.

## ERIC/CASS World Wide Web

This site contains a vast array of resources such as the full-text of all ERIC/CASS Digests and information on upcoming conferences, recent resources added to the ERIC database, professional association activities, new ERIC/CASS publications, etc. It also "hot links" numerous other useful websites such as the U. S. Department of Education, the National Association of School Psychologists, the National Board for Certified Counselors, the NationalCareer Development Association, etc.

## ERIC/CASS ListServs

A unique type of ListServ featuring a "topic of the month" moderated discussion forum with a subject-specialist guest host, ListServs for counselor educators, school psychologist trainers, and school counselors are under development. For full information on the NASP Listserv, use the address (http://www.uncg.edu/~ericcas2/nasp). ListServs for other groups will follow.

# Saving the Native Son: Empowerment Strategies for Young Black Males
## by Courtland C. Lee

**In this greatly expanded and revised edition of the highly acclaimed earlier publication on *Empowering Young Black Males,* Dr. Lee has provided a monograph which is both comprehensive in its coverage (from grades 3 through adolescence) and brimming with practical ideas and interventions. It is a highly thoughtful and probing account of the needs and challenges facing Black youth. It also provides action packed training modules which are unique in the breadth and depth of the activities which they offer. An idea of the richness of the contents can be readily seen by a review of the chapter headings:**

- *The Black Male in Contemporary Society: Social and Educational Challenges*
- *The Psychosocial Development of Black Males: Issues and Impediments*
- *African/American-American Culture: Its Role in the Development of Black Male Youth*
- *"The Young Lions": An Educational Empowerment Program for Black Males in Grades 3-6*
- *"Black Manhood Training": An Empowerment Program for Adolescent Black Males*
- *Tapping the Power of Respected Elders: Ensuring Male Roles Modeling for Black Male Youth*
- *Educational Advocacy for Black Male Students*
- *"S.O.N.S.": Empowerment Strategies for African American Parents*
- *White Men Can't Jump," But Can They be Helpful?*
- *"The Malcolm X Principle": Self-Help for Young Black Males*
- *A Call to Action: A Comprehensive Approach to Empowering Young Black Males*

**Counselors, psychologists, social workers, therapists and teachers will find this an immensely rewarding monograph to read and a highly useful resource for responding to the plight of young Black males. This monograph can be the start of a constructive and effective program for young Black males**

- - - - - - - - - - - - - - - - - - - - - - - - - - - - - - - - - - - - - - - - - - -

Please send me _____ copies of *Saving the Native Son: Empowerment Strategies for Young Black Males*
at **$16.95 each** plus $_____ tax (if applicable) and $_____ shipping/handling for a total cost of $_____

☐ **VIDEO ONLY $19.95**      ☐ **VIDEO AND MONOGRAPH $29.95**

**Method of Payment:**

☐ Check/Money Order enclosed for $ _____
(Make checks payable to CAPS Publications)

☐ Purchase Order #_____ (Minimum $50.00)

☐ Charge to my credit card for $ _____
Visa ☐ MasterCard ☐ Exp. Date ☐☐-☐☐

Account No. _____

Signature _____

Name _____

Company/Div. _____

Address _____

City _____ State _____

Zip _____ Phone _____

**Shipping & Handling Charges:**
Add 10% of subtotal for shipping/handling
       Minimum charge is $2.00
Foreign orders: Add 15% of subtotal
       Minimum charge is $3.00
MI residents add 4% tax. NC residents add 6% tax.
Discounts are available on quantity orders of single titles,
    less 10% for 6-24 copies, less 15% for 25 or more copies.
By Mail:  CAPS Publications
          School of Education, 101 Park Building
          University of North Carolina at Greensboro
          Greensboro, NC  27412-5001
By Phone: Call (910) 334-4114, M-F, 9am-5pm
By FAX: (910) 334-4116

Call about our Book Examination Policy for Classroom Use

# THE ULTIMATE RESOURCE IN CAREER DEVELOPMENT!!

Produced in collaboration with the National Career Development Association

## Career Transitions in Turbulent Times
### Exploring Work, Learning and Careers
Rich Feller & Garry Walz

1996, 557 pages

This unique monograph offers the compelling insights of over fifty knowledgeable authors. In forty seven chapters, they share with the reader important milestones in career development. Particularly noteworthy is the attention devoted to highlighting important new trends and innovations which will shape the future of career development programs and practices for years to come.

The book is divided into six major areas with each area drawing upon the expertise of persons highly knowledgeable in their perception of what is needed and what we currently enjoy. The six areas and the authors in each area are:

### Foundations Revisited

| | | | |
|---|---|---|---|
| Henry Borow | Esther Matthews | Samuel Osipow | Nancy Schlossberg |
| Norman Gysbers | Carl McDaniels | Anna Ranieri | Anna Miller-Tiedeman |
| Sunny Hansen | John McFadden | Lee Richmond | David Tiedeman |
| | John Krumboltz | Larry Osborne | |

### Turbulence in Career Development: What Changes are Occurring in Career Development & Why

| | | | |
|---|---|---|---|
| William Charland | Tom Harrington | Richard Knowdell | George Ritzer |
| Cal Crow | Kenneth Hoyt | Juliette Lester | Jane Walter |
| Rich Feller | Frank Jarlett | Rodney Lowman | A.G. Watts |

### How Career Development is Responding to Different Client Populations

| | | |
|---|---|---|
| Judith Ettinger | Frederic Hudson | Frederick Leong |
| Marian Stoltz-Loike | Edwin Herr | Diane Kjos | Alice Potter |

### Innovative Tools and Techniques That Maximize the Effectiveness of Career Development Interventions

| | | | | |
|---|---|---|---|---|
| David Campbell | Janet Lenz | Robert Reardon | Mary Heppner | |
| Albert Pautler | James Sampson | Ed Jacobs | Gary Peterson | Denise Saunders |

### A Look to the Future of Career Development Programs and Practices

| | | | |
|---|---|---|---|
| Sharon Anderson | Larry Burlew | H.B. Gelatt | Juliet Miller |
| Lynne Bezanson | Beth Durodoye | Bryan Hiebert | Howard Splete |
| JoAnn Bowlsbey | Dennis Engels | Carolyn Kern | Garry Walz |

### A Summing Up and a Leap To the Future
Garry Walz    Rich Feller

### Plus a Special Resources Section!!

(OVER)
153

# Career Transitions in Turbulent Times
## Exploring Work, Learning and Careers

### Editing & Contributions by Rich Feller and Garry Walz

Seldom has one book been able to capture the thinking and recommendations of such a knowledgeable group of writers. Whether career specialist, educator or researcher, the contents of this monograph will surely prove valuable now and for some time to come.

## What Purchasers are Saying:

**Introduced at the ACA Convention in Pittsburg in April, 1996, the monograph won instant acclaim. Here is a sampling of the comments made by enthusiastic purchasers at the ERIC/CASS convention booth:**

- *Just what I've needed for my career development class—highly interesting, very comprehensive and comparatively low-priced!*
- *I'm calling my bookstore now to make it a requirement for my course—even though I authored another book!*
- *I can't believe how comprehensive and current it is. It covers all the new topics I've previously had to scramble to find resources on.*
- *This is just what we needed—broad coverage, focused on implementation and looking forward not backwards.*
- *A winner! I know my students will read and enjoy this. It speaks to things they're interested in!*

---

Please send me ____ copies of *Career Transitions in Turbulent Times: Exploring Work, Learning and Careers* at $29.95 each for a subtotal of $_____ plus shipping and handling (see below) of $ _____ and 6% or 4% sales tax (if applicable) of $ _____ for a total of $ _____ .

### METHOD OF PAYMENT:

☐ Check/Money Order enclosed for $ _____
(Make checks payable to CAPS Publications)

☐ Purchase Order # _____ (minimum $50.00.)

☐ Charge $ _____ to my credit card.

Visa ☐ MasterCard ☐ Exp. Date ☐☐ - ☐☐

Account No. _____

Signature _____

Name _____

Company _____

Address _____

_____

City _____

State _____ Zip _____

Phone _____

### SHIPPING AND HANDLING CHARGES

Add 10% for shipping & handling.
  $2.00 Minimum.
Foreign Orders: add 15%. $3.00 Minimum.
NC residents add 6% sales tax.
MI residents add 4% sales tax.
Discounts are available on quantity
  orders of single titles:
10% for 6-12 copies, 15% for 13-24 copies,
  20% for 25 or more copies.

### HOW TO ORDER:

By Mail: Clip and return with payment to:
  CAPS Publications
  101 Park Building
  University of North Carolina
    at Greensboro
  Greensboro, North Carolina
    27412 - 5001
By Phone: (800) 414-9769
    M-F, (9 am - 4 pm)
By FAX: (910) 334-4116

---

**Please request our Book Examination Policy when considering books for possible classroom use.**

# Two Outstanding Monographs for
## Assisting Students in Coping with Fears, Stress, and Crises

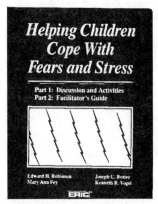

### Helping Children Cope With Fears and Stress

Part 1: Discussion and Activities
Part 2: Facilitator's Guide

*Edward H. Robinson, Joseph C. Rotter, Mary Ann Fey, and Kenneth R. Vogel*

Although learning to deal with stressors is a normal part of growing up, many children develop inadequate or inappropriate coping strategies. Researchers have linked this inability to cope appropriately to the increasing rate of teen and pre-teen suicide, substance abuse, teen pregnancy, and academic failure. Because the consequences of fears and stress are potentially so serious, counselors, teachers, and all educators must be cognizant of the signs of fears and stress among young students, and they must become aware as well of activities and strategies that alleviate or prevent their deleterious effects. This volume includes:

- a concise overview of children's fears and stress

- 47 activities and strategies for individual and group counseling interventions or for easy integration into the K-8 curriculum

- a facilitator's guide detailing an eight-session workshop for training teachers and counselors on how to help children cope with fears and stress

*178 Pages*       Item No. EC188       $16.95

*An ERIC/CASS Publication*

### Developing Support Groups for Students: Helping Students Cope With Crises

*Garry R. Walz and Jeanne C. Bleuer, Editors*

Students of all ages experience directly or indirectly the trauma and stress associated with crime and violence, drug and alcohol abuse, and family disruptions brought about by divorce and parental joblessness. Other events such as the 1991 Persian Gulf war, earthquakes and hurricanes can cause added stress. Developed at the request of the U.S. Department of Education, this volume includes six information-packed modules offering clear instructions for how to utilize the proven power of student support gorups to assist students in developing well-balanced and emotionally stable personalities.

Module 1: **Helping Students Cope With Fears and Crises**

Module 2: **Programs and Practices for Helping Students Cope with Fears and Crises**

Module 3: **Developing and Offering Student Self-Help Support Groups**

Module 4: **Designing and Implementing Student Support Programs**

Module 5: **Abstracts of Significant Resources**

Module 6: **Sources for Assistance and Consultation**

*202 Pages*       Item No. EC188       $16.95

*An ERIC/CASS Publication*

---

SPECIAL OFFER – Order BOTH *Helping Students Cope with Fears and Stress* and *Developing Support Groups for Students* as a set for only $29.90, **a $4.00 savings !!!**

---

Please send me _____ copies of _____ at $_____ each, plus $_____ sales tax, if applicable, and $ _____ shipping/handling for a total cost of $ _____.

Method of Payment
   Check/Money Order enclosed for $ _____
   (Payable to **CAPS Publications**)
   Purchase Order # _____ ($50 minimum)
   Charge my ❑VISA ❑MasterCard for $ _____
   Expiration Date ___ ___ / ___ ___
             Month   Year

Account No. _____
Signature _____
Name _____
Address _____
_____
City _____
State _____ Zip __ __ __ __ __ - __ __ __ __
Phone (_____) _____-_____
FAX (_____) _____-_____

**Shipping/Handling Charges:**
Add 10% of subtotal for shipping/handling
      Minimum charge: $2.00
Foreign orders: Add 15% of subtotal
      Minimum charge: $3.00
**NC residents add 6% sales tax.**
**Quantity Discounts: 6-24 10%; 25 or more 15%**
**By Mail:  CAPS Publications**
        School of Education, Park 101
        University of North Carolina
          at Greensboro
        Greensboro, NC 27412-5001
**By Phone:** (800) 414-9769  9a.m.-5p.m., EST
**By FAX:**   (910) 334-4116
    **Call about our Book Examination Policy !!**

Item No. EC 199    $19.95

# Counseling Employment Bound Youth

## Edwin L. Herr Ed.D.

Distinguished Professor of Education and Associate Dean
for Academic Programs and Research
The Pennsylvania State University

At long last, we have the monograph which so many persons have needed and sought out for such a long period of time—*Counseling Employment-Bound Youth*. Employment bound youth, a large and vital segment of our population (20 million plus) and future labor force, have been largely ignored in the literature on careers and on counseling and guidance. This neglect has clearly been to the great detriment not only of the young people themselves but to our country's vitality and competitiveness in the rapidly expanding global economy.

In seven vital and compelling chapters, Dr. Herr covers the topics which make this monograph both a thought piece and a practical handbook. The basic topics covered are:

- *Employment-bound youth: Diversity in characteristics, opportunities and support*

- *The emerging economic investment for employment-bound youth*

- *Career development for employment-bound youth in schools*

- *The school-to-work transition for employment-bound youth*

- *Career counseling for employment-bound youth*

- *The counselor and related career interventions*

- *Epilogue—Challenges to and the future of career counseling and guidance*

In masterful writing that offers a broad and comprehensive overview of the challenges faced as well as specific recommendations for how school, business, and communities can and should respond, Dr. Herr has produced a thoughtful yet eminently practical book. This compelling monograph is directed towards counselors, career specialists, teachers, administrators, policy makers and community members who are desirous of providing practical assistance to employment bound youth.

*"This is the most comprehensive and best researched publication on career development in existence! It is a landmark publication for counseling and career development. Both educators and practitioners will find it eminently useful and applicable to what they do."*
Kenneth Hoyt
Distinguished Professor of Education
Kansas State University

*" Ed Herr is our pre-eminent writer on career development today. In this masterful book, he provides a comprehensive and detailed look at the needs of the employment bound and how counselors and career specialists can help them. I strongly recommend this book to anyone who is interested in the school-to-work transition and employment bound youth."*
Norman C. Gysbers
Professor
University of Missouri

CONTENTS OF
# Counseling Employment Bound Youth

- Employment-bound youth: Diversity in characteristics, opportunities and support
- The emerging economic investment for employment-bound youth
- Career development for employment-bound youth in schools
- The school-to-work transition for employment-bound youth
- Career counseling for employment-bound youth
- The counselor and related career interventions
- Epilogue—Challenges to and the future of career counseling and guidance

- - - - - - - - - - - - - - - - - - - - - - - - - - - - - - - - - -

Please send me____copies of *Counseling Employment Bound Youth* at $19.95 each for a subtotal of $_____ plus shipping and handling (see below) of $_____ and 6% or 4% sales tax (if applicable) of $_____ for a total of $_____.

METHOD OF PAYMENT:

☐ Check/Money Order enclosed for $_____.
(Make checks payable to CAPS Publications)

☐ Purchase Order # _____ (minimum $50.00.)

☐ Charge $ _____ to my credit card.

Visa ☐ MasterCard ☐ Exp. Date ☐☐ - ☐☐

Account No. _____

Signature _____

Name _____

Company _____

Address _____

_____

City _____

State _____ Zip _____

Phone _____

SHIPPING AND HANDLING CHARGES

Add 10% for shipping & handling. $2.00 Minimum.
Foreign Orders: add 15%. $3.00 Minimum.
NC residents add 6% sales tax.
MI residents add 4% sales tax.
Discounts are available on quantity orders of single titles:
10% for 6-12 copies, 15% for 13-24 copies, 20% for 25 or more copies.

HOW TO ORDER:

By Mail: Clip and return with payment to:
CAPS Publications
101 Park Building
University of North Carolina at Greensboro
Greensboro, North Carolina
27412 - 5001
By Phone: (800) 414-9769
M-F, (9 am - 4 pm)
By FAX: (910) 334-4116

Please request our Book Examination Policy when considering books for possible classroom use.